Documentary Film

Documentary Film

✦

A Primer

Carl Rollyson

iUniverse, Inc.
New York Lincoln Shanghai

Documentary Film
A Primer

iUniverse books may be ordered through booksellers or by contacting:

iUniverse
2021 Pine Lake Road, Suite 100
Lincoln, NE 68512
www.iuniverse.com
1-800-Authors (1-800-288-4677)

ISBN: 0-595-33925-5

Printed in the United States of America

Contents

A Primer

Documentary film is a form of reporting about the world. Like a newspaper, a documentary provides information about events, people, places, and virtually any subject of interest to the public. In words and pictures, documentaries show us what has happened, or is still happening, in our world. Whether we watch a documentary about a war or a biography of a famous figure, we presume that we are absorbing a presentation of fact.

Of course, documentaries are no such thing: to assemble a film—or a newspaper for that matter—is an act of interpretation. What should the headline be? Which photographs appear on the front page? Whose story will be featured? These are all editorial decisions. Like newspapers, films are edited. Stories get left out or shortened. In a film, scenes are shot from certain angles. Interviews with subjects are reshaped to fit the framework of film.

There is an opening sequence of a documentary about Lillian Hellman in which the phrases from several interviews are merged into shots of several speakers who seem to be contributing to one succinct statement about the film's subject. The film has thus created a dialogue between the speakers that in fact never occurred.

Is such a film dishonest? No, because documentaries are inevitably interpretations; the documentarian, like a newspaper editor, is picking and choosing the items that suit the film's style and point of view. Hellman, a controversial figure, demands the solicitation of many perspectives, and yet, the filmmaker implies, those perspectives can be melded into a unified statement.

The very earliest films lacked this kind of coherent vision. They simply put a stationary camera in front of what was to be recorded. In part, the stationary camera simply reflected the state of technology. As cameras became lighter in weight or were mounted on rails or wheels, so that they could move with the action, filmmakers became more selective—or rather, camera movement by definition meant that interpretation, as well as reportage, became possible.

As soon as the camera could move, filmmakers had their choice of close-ups and medium and long shots. Better lenses meant the human face could be brought closer to the audience's eye than faces that appeared outside of film. Film

1

stimulated an involvement with the human figure that was unprecedented. A face—just the face—could occupy an entire screen; a close-up could fasten on a hand making an expressive gesture. And what could be shown of figures could also be shown of objects—of anything that was susceptible to the camera's scrutiny.

The expanded technological resources of film had an aesthetic and moral result: film became, in a sense, its own reality. Rather than just reporting on the world; it created a world. Film was still a document but of a very peculiar kind.

Montage, the juxtapositions of different images on pieces or frames of film, can in itself create meaning. Thus a man with tears in his eyes might appear either sad or happy depending on the images that preceded and succeeded the shot of him crying. One can, after all, cry with joy or sorrow. Reverse the succeeding and preceding images and the interpretation of the man's emotions changes.

Cameras and the editing of what cameras record can also speed up or slow down the action of a scene. For example, in *Olympia*, Leni Riefenstahl's camera lovingly tracks in slow motion the athlete's ascent over the bar in the pole-vaulting event. We have an intimate and prolonged attachment to the athlete unavailable to the spectators in the Olympic stadium. This kind of shot excites the viewer, who is enjoying a privileged point of view. Riefenstahl's style is seductive. She wants her audience to revel in the beauty and suppleness of the human form. Although she is recording an event, she is also creating a kind of poem.

This development of film as a way of not only knowing the world but of creating and enjoying it is reminiscent of William Wordsworth's famous statement that we half-perceive and half-create our universe. We do not merely see the world; we project our sense of how it impinges on us. Projection, of course, is the perfect word for film. It projects a world and in the process changes it.

This is what filmmaker Robert Flaherty discovered when he decided to film the Inuit people in Canada's Hudson Bay region. He began by simply doing a travelogue, recording the manners and customs of a culture that he hoped would not only appeal to the curiosity of filmgoers but also cause them to reflect on the temper of modern life. The Inuits lived in the raw, so to speak, without labor saving devices and the array of inventions that included, of course, the movie camera. But Flaherty found he could not simply record Inuit life. For one thing, their way of life had changed by the time Flaherty showed up. They had abandoned many traditional customs and no longer hunted, for example, with bow and arrow. Inuits had guns.

What to do? Flaherty actually helped the Inuits to recover their old ways of doing things. So we see Nanook in *Nanook of the North* hunting without the aid of firearms. Flaherty also includes a scene in which Nanook teaches his child how to use a bow and arrow. The scene is charming but in a sense false. The child will not grow up to hunt in this way. The traditional life the film purports to record was in fact fast disappearing.

Is Flaherty, then, a fraud? Well, the people he films are real. The actions they perform were once a part of Inuit life. How else to show what that life had been without re-enacting scenes that evoked a past way of life? It could be argued that Flaherty was engaging in an act of restoration or restitution, showing not only his audience but also the Inuits themselves a way of life that would otherwise be left unrecorded.

Documentary film, after all, stems from an urge to commemorate, to honor the lives of others. But the filmgoer should never forget that film is a medium, a means of conveyance, and even of transformation, not the thing itself. This is Dziga Vertov's point in *Man with the Movie Camera*. We see scenes of the Soviet Union in 1929, but the film repeatedly reminds us that they are all "shot," captured in the camera eye, edited in a studio, and scored with a sound track that seems to build and build in tempo and yet never quite comes to a resolution. The film itself is unresolved—as if the filmmaker is resisting the very seductiveness of the medium, making us realize, again and again, that we are watching a movie.

Woody Allen aims at a similar self-conscious examination of the documentary in *Zelig*. Critic Susan Sontag, together with Nobel prize-winning novelist Saul Bellow, child psychiatrist Bruno Bettelheim, critic Irving Howe, and Professor John Morton Blum, were chosen, Allen said, to endow his film with the "patina of intellectual weight and seriousness." This group of notables provide commentary on the bizarre career of Leonard Zelig, who could change color, body shape, even ethnic and national identity, blending into whatever company he sought. In mock-documentary mode, with voice-over narration, expert testimony, and faked photographs, Allen superbly constructed an amalgam of *Citizen Kane* and *Reds*—with Zelig also acting a kind of Jay Gatsby figure.

It is as if Allen were illustrating the thesis of *On Photography*, in which Sontag argued that photographs are not real but surreal precisely because they can fuse features that do not belong together into one credible image. Photographs, she contended, had become the standard measure of reality. Allen satirizes the authority of photographs as documents when he pictures Zelig on a medical table surrounded by nurses. Everyone in the shot looks at the camera, and moviegoers look at Zelig, sitting up, his feet sticking out of his hospital gown and rotated so that his heels are up where his toes should be—in other words, he has somehow been able to twist his legs so that the back is now the front and vice versa. (The very difficulty of making this description clear emphasizes how quickly we can take in a photograph as "real," as making sense, even when it is patently false).

Allen's elaborate joke addressed Sontag's deplatonized world, in which we no longer refer the image to the idea; instead, the image itself becomes the source of truth. Similarly, the efforts of psychiatrists to cure Zelig are a send-up of modern psychology, another one of Sontag's *bete noires*. Here she is assessing the role of Eudora Fletcher (Mia Farrow), who not only becomes Zelig's psychiatrist, but his lover and wife:

As she talks to the offscreen interviewer, the caption SUSAN SONTAG, AUTHOR OF *Against Interpretationpops on the screen.*

> SUSAN SONTAG I don't know if you could call it a triumph of psycho-therapy—it seems more like a triumph of aesthetic instincts. (*Gesturing*) Because Dr. Fletcher's techniques didn't owe anything to then current schools of therapy. But she sensed what was needed and she provided it, and that was, in its way, a remarkable creative accomplishment.

The "triumph of aesthetic instincts," is a quintessential Susan Sontag phrase—although she could not have known how the film mimicked her own work, since Allen did not give his intellectual stars scripts. They were not even told what the film was about; rather, they were part of the process of intellectualizing that Allen satirized. Perhaps that is why Saul Bellow later complained that he felt he had been made to look foolish.

Allen's shrewdness is also revealed in his decision to have Sontag open the film. She is first heard in a voice-over: "He was <u>the</u> phenomenon of the…" Then there is a cut to

> *The present day, in living color. Susan Sontag is sitting at an outdoor cafe, a coffee cup in front of her. She faces the camera, still talking, as behind her an idyllic glimpse of Venice is seen: a bright blue sky, gondolas on the canal, sea gulls flying by the slanted roofs. Her name pops on the bottom of the screen:* SUSAN SONTAG.

SUSAN SONTAG (*Continuing, fingering her napkin*)…twenties. When you think that at that time he was as well known as Lindbergh, it's really quite astonishing.

Like the other intellectual stars—except perhaps Bellow—Sontag seems to be enjoying herself. She looks cheerful, as if she is about to break out in a grin, as if she knows that you know that she knows this is all camp, and as if she is pleased to be one of the four featured intellectual luminaries.

Zelig's comment on the documentary form is devastating. Virtually every technique the documentarian uses, the film demonstrates, can be applied to a fictional subject. In other words, there is nothing "real" or "authentic" about documentary at all. It is simply, like all film, a style of representation.

Some years ago a filmmaker produced a film about a small town facing the devastating loss of an important corporation, which had decided to move its headquarters to another part of the country. The film presented interviews with townspeople, businessmen, politicians, and in general portrayed a community in crisis. Those reviewers who walked out at the end of the film without seeing the credits wrote about the film as a documentary. What they missed was the statement in the credits that revealed the film was entirely a work of fiction. There was no such town; the story was made up.

Does this mean that all film is a fake, a lie? Plato thought so—not about film but about artists, who created, in his view, deceptive works that deflected our attention from the "real world." And yet, as Samuel Taylor Coleridge argued, art moves us as if it is real. We cry and laugh and identify with characters, and we would be very cross if someone stood up in a theater and yelled it was all a counterfeit.

Oscar Wilde long ago contended that art was a lie that told the truth. This paradox is at the heart of all art, including documentary film. The extent to which we can identify the artfulness of documentary is also the extent to which we can take its measure as truth. All art manipulates; the point is to understand the process and the techniques of manipulation.

Warren Beatty's *Reds*, the story of John Reed and Louise Bryant—lovers and journalists who reported on the Russian Revolution is a telling exploration of art as lie and truth. Beatty plays Reed with romantic bravado. Diana Keaton projects a confused yet committed Bryant. Although the film is no documentary, it attempts to explore the nature of historical truth by intercutting scenes with the reminiscences of people who knew Reed and Bryant. These witnesses struggle to recall events, sometime misremembering or even forgetting much of the period they are supposed to be explaining. What seems so magnetic and persuasive in the Reed-Bryant story is thus subjected to doubt.

On the other hand, the voices of historical figures provide an authentic weight to Warren Beatty's film. It is as if he is saying, "Look at how hard I tried to explore history, to meld my story out of conflicting points of view." Both film's strengths and limitations are admirably stressed in this part fiction/part documentary work.

Susan Sontag, one of Oscar Wilde's modern-day acolytes, has explored as well as anyone the dilemma that documentary film presents: what is its truth-value? To what extent can we admire a film for its style even if we find its "truth" repugnant?

On February 6, 1975 *The New York Review of Books* published "Fascinating Fascism," Sontag's full-scale assault on the rehabilitation of Leni Riefenstahl, best known for her Nazi-era documentaries, *Triumph of the Will* and *Olympia*. As Sontag confided to her publisher Roger Straus, she had written the piece to make a "splash"—which it did, provoking lavish praise and fierce criticism, as well as a high volume of letters that Sontag relished. Robert Silvers, editor of *The New York Review of Books*, told her that that particular issue of NYR had been one of their best sellers.

Sontag began by evoking the beautiful—indeed ravishing—photographs in Riefenstahl's recent book, *The Last of the Nuba*. But then she meticulously set out to destroy the Riefenstahl persona, showing how the filmmaker had lied about her Nazi affiliations and how her publisher and film critics had collaborated in her elisions of history, which made her out to be an artist first, a propagandist second. Riefenstahl portrayed herself as a German Romantic who had the misfortune of attracting Hitler's attention but who had been acquitted twice of any complicity in war crimes. The beautiful Riefenstahl—Sontag made much of the way Riefenstahl had been photographed—this "character," as Sontag put it, "underwent a steady aggrandizement." It seemed to nettle Sontag that Riefenstahl billed herself as an independent filmmaker when, in fact, she had been bankrolled by Hitler, who had made his Nuremberg rallies into a movie set for her.

Had Sontag halted her blitzkrieg at this point, her essay would have kicked up a fuss mainly in the film world and among literary critics interested to find that she had reversed course. There had been that notorious passage in *Against Interpretation*, in which Sontag had cautioned that merely to condemn Riefenstahl for her reprehensible Nazi content would be to diminish the vital experience of artistic form. Sontag knew quite well that "Fascinating Fascism" might be viewed as a repudiation of her earlier remarks, and she had her answer ready when Robert Boyers (a friend) gave her a forum in *Salmagundi* (Fall/Winter 1975/76) to say that she had not contradicted herself so much as she had looked at the form/content distinction from a different angle. She had been concerned in the earlier essay to emphasize form because critics seemed obsessed with content. What mattered, Sontag argued, was context; it troubled her that *only* form had become the issue as Riefenstahl and her promoters ignored or excused her Nazi past. And what of Sontag's own role in shaping the taste for form that she now repudiated? "The hard truth is that what may be acceptable in elite culture may not be acceptable in mass culture, that taste which poses only innocuous ethical issues as the property of a minority becomes corrupting when they become more established" Sontag concludes.

Sontag had changed (she admitted in *Salmagundi*) insofar as she had a "much denser notion of historical context," which led her to speculate on other reasons for Riefenstahl's rehabilitation. Surely the "fact that she is a woman" helped turn her into a "cultural monument." Here Sontag knew she had touched a nerve—one that she irritated further by claiming that feminists had embraced the beautiful Leni because of her status as one of the few world class female filmmakers. To rile feminists even more, Sontag emphasized the demeaning nature of Riefenstahl's fascist aesthetic: it glorified submission to an all-powerful leader. Indeed, it was pornographic in its exultation in the triumph of the strong over the weak, turning people into things, celebrating the primitive, the virile, making a cult and a fetish of beauty. This fascist aesthetic had become fashionable, a part of the camp sensibility, Sontag said, setting off echoes of the essay that had first brought her fame. A liberal culture, she opined, revolved around cycles of taste; it was simply fascism's turn on the "cultural wheel."

Poet Adrienne Rich wrote NYR (March 20, 1975) in shock. Was this the author of "The Third World of Women"? That essay, which argued that true change would come only when women forced men to share power, had inspired Rich to watch how Sontag would work her "lucid and beautifully reasoned" insights into her subsequent work. But "Fascinating Fascism" was full of "failed connections." It was so inimical to "The Third World of Women" that Rich wondered if that essay had been, "after all, more of an intellectual exercise than the expression of a felt reality—her own—interpreted by a keen mind." Why blame women for Riefenstahl's rehabilitation? Wasn't it mainly the work of cineastes? And why end the discussion of Riefenstahl with general comments about liberal society and its fads? Why not make the connection between "patriarchal history, sexuality, pornography, and power"? Why not explain how the passivity induced by ideologies such as fascism was always linked to female qualities? Not to demonstrate that the first people turned into things were always women, not to show that women's minds and bodies were always the first to be colonized, was to practice a "kind of dissociation of one kind of knowledge from another which reinforces cultism and aesthetic compromise with the representatives of oppression; precisely what Sontag herself was writing to deplore."

One Sontag friend remembers that Rich's letter devastated Sontag, and that it was an agony for her to compose a reply. In another mood, Sontag wrote a staff member at her publisher Farrar, Straus & Giroux: "I counter-attacked. What else could I do?" Sontag dismissed Rich as a commissar enforcing a party line—although Rich had stated she was *not* looking for a 'line.' "Sontag scored against Rich for using terms like "male-identified 'successful' women," to compose an "ominous-sounding enemies list." Did Sontag have to mention feminism in everything she wrote? Was all history to be reduced to discussions of the patriarchy? "Like all capital moral truths, feminism is a bit simple-minded," she concluded. Most of history was, "alas, 'patriarchal history.' " But how to distinguish between one patriarch and another, one period of history and another? Rich's brand of feminism, in other words, was reductive in its demand for "unremitting rhetoric, with every argument arriving triumphantly at a militant conclusion."

Of course, that was the freight train of feminism Sontag rode in "The Third World of Women." Why should Sontag have been offended that Rich wanted to know where Sontag's apparently uncompromising feminism was headed? Instead, Sontag turned the occasion of her reply into a diatribe against programmatic feminists and into a defense of Elizabeth Hardwick, whose book, *Seduction and Betrayal*, had been discounted by feminists. Sontag claimed that Hardwick's work had been discounted because it had been regarded as too elitist, too taken with talent and genius, and insufficiently respectful of the movement's egalitarian ethics. In other words, Rich and her ilk were vulgarians, leftovers from the "infantile leftism of the 1960s." (There was no acknowledgement here of the Sontag who had contributed her share of Marxist simplicities to the period, and who had ended a piece on Cuban poster art by exclaiming "Viva Fidel.") For Rich history was no more than shallow psychology, Sontag suggested.

Sontag ended her rebuttal by refusing to take up Rich's personal challenge. In effect, Rich was asking Sontag: "Come on, what do you really *feel* about feminism?" Sontag sought the high ground: "Although I defy anyone to read what I wrote and miss its personal, even autobiographical character, I much prefer that the text be judged as an argument and not as an 'expression' of anything at all, my sincere feelings included."

But "Fascinating Fascism" is a fascinating study of Sontag. The parallels with Riefenstahl are obvious: both women trade on their images, on making sure they photograph well. Both filmmakers, they know all about manipulating their images even as they vehemently deny that they do so. They both submit to powerful male promoters. They both get caught up in revolutionary rhetoric and in the cult of the maximum leader. "Viva Fidel!" is the Communist version of "Heil Hitler!" Indeed, in "Fascinating Fascism" Sontag delineates a number of parallels between the aesthetics of fascism and communism. In both, the "will is staged publicly." Castro's public, operatic theater—the idea of a whole society mobilized by his rhetoric—thrilled Sontag. Here is Sontag quoting Riefenstahl, but Sontag might as well be quoting herself: the "care for composition, the aspiration to form...Whatever is purely realistic, slice-of-life, which is average, quotidian, doesn't interest me."

Riefenstahl remains forever a Nazi in "Fascinating Fascism." Her pre-Nazi films, which emphasize the cult of the body, are treated as precursors of fascist aesthetics. Sontag ignores how Riefenstahl is using the pictorial devices of the German Romantics and the literary themes of Novalis, Tieck, Goethe, von Eichendorff, and Holderlin. By ignoring both form and context Sontag denies Riefenstahl's development as an artist and the evolution of her ideology—a point several film critics have made about "Fascinating Fascism."

The animus between Riefenstahl and Sontag continues. In *Leni Riefenstahl: A Memoir* (1992), Riefenstahl attacks Sontag for her lack of objectivity, mentioning but not naming journalists who have disputed Sontag's statement of the facts. In the spring of 1995, Riefenstahl was invited to the San Francisco Film Festival, a part of the highly successful City Arts & Lectures series, at which Sontag has often appeared. Riefenstahl, then 92, wrote to say she could not come because—as columnist Herb Caen reported—the "tough old bird" had injured herself scuba diving. The trip would have been called off anyway, though, because the eight member committee (mainly Jewish) responsible for inviting Riefenstahl included, according to Caen in *The San Francisco Chronicle* (March 30, 1995), one vociferous dissenter: "Susan Sontag, another tough bird."

It would be misleading, however, to simply equate Sontag and Riefenstahl. If Sontag has been attracted to power and to the powerful male, she has also been critical of both. Sontag was horrified at how much Riefenstahl's decades-long denial of her complicity in evil had degraded her ability to be an artist and had corrupted her. "Fascinating Fascism," then, has to be regarded as Sontag's first step in her public recantation of a politics that excused Communist tyranny and the cult, especially in Cuba, of the "maximum leader."

A Case Study: Jill Craigie (1911–1999)

"British Filmmaker and Socialist, Dies at 85," *The New York Times* announced on December 18, 1999. The obituary called Jill Craigie a feminist and observed that her "half-century marriage to Labor Party Leader Michael Foot put her at the heart of the country's leftist politics." Craigie's life unfolded in overlapping phases. After years in boarding schools that resembled those places of confinement in Charlotte Bronte's novels, Craigie emerged in World War II London as a pioneering documentary filmmaker—the first woman director to attract national attention. She combined an outspoken socialism and a concern for the aesthetics of modern life with a determination to tell the story of the modern women's movement.

In 1944, Craigie encountered the survivors of the suffragette generation who had gathered at the statue of their great leader, Emmeline Pankhurst. Craigie befriended and interviewed these women, then sought funding for a film that ultimately could not be made in wartime London. Instead, she produced *Out of Chaos* (1944), one of the first documentaries about modern art—featuring Henry Moore, Graham Sutherland, Stanley Spencer, and Paul Nash. Craigie put Kenneth Clark on camera for the first time, directing him in a style that he would later use for *Civilization*, his groundbreaking television series about art.

In 1945, Craigie met Michael Foot, then conducting his first campaign for Parliament. In her film, *The Way We Live* (1946), Foot's speech to the people of Plymouth epitomizes the spirit of the British Labour Party in the historic election that would determine how postwar Britain was to be rebuilt. Craigie and Foot would become a political team. In *Diaries of a Cabinet Minister* (1975), Richard Crossman wrote that Craigie fought for her husband like a tiger; she was not merely interested in politics; she was a politician herself. A forceful presence in the debate about Britain's quality of life and its place in the world, she engaged in the campaign for unilateral nuclear disarmament. She also wrote screenplays, articles, and her crowning achievement, *Daughters of Dissent*, a magisterial history of the drive for women's rights nearly completed at the time of her death. *Daughters of Dissent*, along with *Two Hours From London* (1994), Craigie's searing documentary on the siege of Dubrovnik, constitute the legacy of a writer, filmmaker, and political activist who kept enlarging the scope of what it means to be a twentieth-century woman.

Craigie's six decades of involvement with women's issues provides a virtual barometer of changes in social and political attitudes both in Great Britain and in the world at large. She tried to integrate her feminism into every aspect of her life. Even as she was involved in the air raid alert system in wartime London (making sure people got to shelters during the bombing), she was trying to get financing for her film on the suffragettes. When she could not obtain funding for her film, she turned instead to a radio documentary on the suffragettes, broadcast in 1950 as "The Woman's Rebellion." In 1951, she directed a film documentary, *To Be a Woman* (1951), a forceful feminist plea for equal pay for equal work. In the 1950s she protested the threat of nuclear war in public speeches that included an impassioned protest against the dangers of radiation. Citing such risks as birth defects, she spoke as a mother and feminist, making the issue of nuclear proliferation a woman's issue. At the same time, of course, she campaigned fiercely within the Labour Party for a whole range of issues—including public housing, which she thought should be organically tied to human communities so that the classes intermingled in a setting reminiscent of the traditional village green. She had an aesthetic aspiration to make people's lives vivid and rewarding. Inspired by her friend, Lewis Mumford, and her mentor, the great Labour Party Leader Aneurin Bevan (another Mumford admirer), Craigie portrayed the need for town planning in her documentary, *The Way We Live*, which featured the "Plymouth Plan," designed to rebuild the city and to draw all classes of the community together. Craigie was part of a generation of political women—including Michael Foot's close friend and Labour Party colleague, Barbara Castle, who called themselves "William Morris Socialists." Like the Victorian domestic polymath, they appreciated such matters as the need to craft pattern and color into the forms and structures of everyday life. It was precisely this impulse that prompted Craigie to direct the television documentary, *Who Are the Vandals?* (1967), an excoriation of housing developers who had ruined a good deal of the English landscape.

In the 1970s, energized by the women's movement Craigie began her epic book about the drive for female enfranchisement, beginning in the middle of the 19th century and climaxing with the great suffragette agitation directly preceding World War I. Her impressively documented study relies on a deep reading of secondary sources as well as on the copious primary evidence she had begun collecting in the 1940s with her interviews with suffragettes. Craigie's book is also a disguised autobiography: *Daughters of Dissent* explores the complex interaction of women's issues, the demands of the labour movement, and the development of modern political parties and their constituencies from the perspective of a woman who had access to Cabinet Ministers and Prime Ministers and campaigned along-side her husband in his quest for high office. In 1975, through the intervention of her husband, then a Cabinet Secretary in the Harold Wilson government, Craigie obtained new records about the treatment of suffragettes in British prisons, records previously sequestered under the Official Secrets Act.

Also in the 1970s, Craigie became actively involved in the founding of Virago Press. Indeed, Craigie, who brought back into print a good deal of the texts now important to the discipline of women's studies, first suggested many of this feminist publisher's titles. Countless scholars in the field can testify to Craigie's encouragement of their work as well as to her critical, demanding judgment that women's studies must produce new data and give due credit both to militants such as Emmeline Pankhurst and to gradualists or more reform-minded figures such as Millicent Fawcett. And indeed, *Daughters of Dissent* explores the conflicting but also complementary roles of these two great figures and their families. The stories of the Pankhursts and the Fawcetts form the spine of Craigie's book. And the same dramatic contrast between these feminist dynasties also forms the basis of a musical comedy and a film script that Craigie left in her papers.

In the 1980s and 1990s, Craigie became increasingly involved in a study of Yugoslavia. For the last 15 years of her life, she traveled to Dubrovnik at least once each year with her husband, who had formed a close relationship with Milovan Djilas (who stayed in London with Foot and Craigie when Tito allowed him to travel). Inspired by her friendship with Rebecca West, the author of the *Black Lamb and Grey Falcon*—still the greatest book ever written about Yugoslavia and the fate of Central Europe—Craigie would resume her career as documentary filmmaker, completing *Two Hours From London* (1994), a stinging indictment of the West's failure to intervene in the wars in Yugoslavia. The story of the making of this remarkable film is fully told in *To Be A Woman: The Life of Jill Craigie*.

Jill Craigie died in 1999, just two chapters short of completing her masterpiece, *Daughters of Dissent*.

Out of Chaos

Jill Craigie's career as a documentary filmmaker is a striking contrast to the Sontag/Riefenstahl nexus and the argument over aesthetic form and politics. Her first documentary, *Out of Chaos*, arose out of the powerful yearning of wartime Britain to preserve and perpetuate its art. Public figures such as the great economist John Maynard Keynes (1883-1946) and Kenneth Clark (1903-1983), director of the National Gallery, worked tirelessly to ensure that "'culture' should not be put aside for the duration: in the act of fighting to save England, English culture should not be sacrificed. Clark became the primary force behind the War Artists' Scheme, which produced almost six thousand works of art distributed to museums across the country.

Virtually every museum, cinema, theatre, and concert hall closed at the start of the war, except the National Gallery, which sponsored one-hour afternoon chamber music concerts (admission price, one shilling). For five days a week—from 10 October 1939 to10 April 1946, the museum presented concerts attended by as many as 1,750 people daily for a total of 824,152 over a six-year period. *Out of Chaos* would tell their story, so to speak, by embodying a vision of what art should represent in a democratic, socialist society. For the film arose out an almost palpable feeling that the creation of a socialist society was imminent. As Craigie later said:

> the war suited me very well...it was the nearest to a socialist society we've ever had, and there were all these discussions going on [of art and politics]. You couldn't spend a lot of money on clothes, you couldn't buy furniture, you couldn't buy crockery, you'd got no petrol for the car.... If you listened to [J. B.] Priestley's broadcasts, it was all on the Merrie England that was going to follow under a socialist society, much like the Clarion newspaper during the First World War.

The story of a people coming together through art seemed to Craigie the fulfillment of William Morris's socialist dream. He evolved his vision in a series of lectures to artists and craftsman in London, Birmingham, Oxford, and in many other parts of England from 1877 to 1896. Craigie often recommended these lectures because of their continuing relevance: "I thought you can't have a socialist society unless the socialists themselves study their Morris and Ruskin…. Read his lectures and other writings, he is very, very modern."

Morris (1834-1896)—architect, designer, printer, poet, novelist, and social reformer, a man who made his own furniture, wall paper, textiles, ceramics, and stained glass as well as many other kinds of everyday handcrafted objects inspired by a profound reverence for the artisans of the Middle Ages—seemed supremely important to Craigie during the war, when, as Humphrey Jennings wrote, London had again become a big village in which barriers and partitions and prejudices were breaking down:

> London—to look at it—has settled down to a big village-like existence. Most of the damage demolished and cleared up. Endless allotments—beds of potatoes, onions, lettuces—in parks, in the new open spaces from bombing, tomatoes climbing up ruins—trees and shrubs overgrowing evacuated and empty houses and gardens—in some places shells of eighteenth century cottages with black blank windows and Rousseau-like forests enveloping them, straying out over the road—no railings—climbing in windows. Elsewhere the utmost tidiness and care in lines of planting on AA gunsites, aerodromes, firestations. The parks and squares open to all—all railings gone, shelters overgrown….

Without this collapse of divisions between one class and another, and between one art and another, modern civilization, Morris argues, is doomed. He attacks the distinction between the craftsman and the artist by defining art in this inclusive fashion: "everything made by man's hands has a form, which must be either beautiful or ugly." To live a full life is to recognize the beauty of form in painting or in a knife and fork. Yet cities like London are desecrated with "hideous streets," "ugly surroundings," and the "brutality of squalor." London has its museums, Morris acknowledges, but art (an appreciation of form) has become so divorced from the common experience of people that art itself needs help:

> people need some preliminary instruction before they can get all the good possible to be got from the prodigious treasures of art possessed by the country in that form: there also one sees things in a piecemeal way: nor can I deny that there is something melancholy in a museum, such a tale of violence, destruction, and carelessness, as its treasured scraps tell us.

In *Out of Chaos*, Craigie sets out to cure precisely this sense of alienation from works of art, this inability to "read" art because it exists only in the fragmentary form of a museum.

Morris exhorts his audiences to embrace the older part of the English country-side, where the "works of man" and nature seem to grow out of each other, and where people hold on to the history that urban life so rapidly removes:

> when we think what a small part of the world's history, past, present, and to come, is this land we live in, and how much smaller still in the history of the arts, and yet how our forefathers clung to it, and with what care and pains they adorned it, this unromantic uneventful-look-ing land of England, surely by this too our hearts may be touched, and our hope quickened.

In the land of forefathers, high art and peasant art were part of a continuum tend-ing toward, Morris emphasizes, "*general capability in dealing with the arts.*"

No art can exist unless all the arts "hang together"—a Morris motto that could have been inscribed at the entrance to the wartime afternoon concerts at the National Gallery. All the arts, moreover, are fused in his conception of labour: "what is an artist but a workman who is determined that, whatever else happens, his work shall be excellent? Or, to put it in another way: the decoration of worksmanship, what is it but the expression of man's pleasure in successful labour?" The utilitarian and the aesthetic are not at odds in Morris's program: "nothing can be a work of art which is not useful; that is to say, which does not minister to the body when well under command of the mind, or which does not amuse, soothe, or elevate the mind in a healthy state." He sees no reason why art cannot "make our streets as beautiful as the woods."

In the age of industry and urban expansion, of commerce and what Morris calls the "counting house," art has come to be regarded as a "foolish accident of civilization—nay, worse, perhaps, a nuisance, a disease, a hindrance to human progress." Men narrow their minds to science and politics and business and looked upon art as "at best trifling." Yet what we know of past civilizations, Mor-ris counters, is through their art. And even in the most oppressive eras "daily labour was sweetened by the daily creation of Art." Nowadays, Morris laments, people of all classes are losing that daily sense of art: "I have never been in any rich man's house which would not have looked the better for having a bonfire made outside of it of nine-tenths of all that it held." Machine made objects impose a uniformity and demand intolerable working conditions that anyone with an aesthetic sensibility immediately rejects: "how can we bear to use, how can we enjoy something which has been a pain and grief for the maker to make?"

In place of the daily experience of art and delight in the hand-crafted object, modern culture prizes "luxuries," often demanding the sacrifices of masses and classes of men to satisfy the appetites of a few stimulated by the "hurrying blindness of civilization." The danger, Morris warns, is that "civilization will destroy the beauty of life." Morris urges, in lecture after lecture, that "this wrong of the mass of men being regardless of art was *not* always so," and that "down to very recent days everything that the hand of man touched was more or less beautiful: so that in those days all people who made anything shared in art, as well as all people who used the things so made: that is *all* people shared in art."

Here is the direction Morris gave to Craigie as she began to work on her first documentary: "You cannot educate, you cannot civilize men, unless you can give them a share in art." It would be hard to do, since Morris admits that most men do not miss art in their lives. That said, he issues a call to action and an injunction to the individual:

> No man has any right to say that all has been done for nothing, that all the faithful unwearying strife of those that have gone before us shall lead us nowhither; that mankind will but go round and round in a circle for ever; no man has a right to say that, and then get up morning after morning to eat his victuals and sleep a-nights, all the while making other people toil to keep his worthless life a-going.

What is true for the individual is also true for all: the "civilization which does not carry the whole people with it is doomed to fall." Think of reading Morris during the Blitz when London may have seemed on its way to being leveled: "And of course mere cheating and flunky centres like the horrible muck-heap in which we dwell (London, to wit) could be got rid of easier still; and a few pleasant villages on the side of the Thames might mark the place of that preposterous piece of folly once called London."

Here then is the problem for the documentary filmmaker Craigie set herself to become: how to carry all the people with her, to produce that sense of everyone sharing in art, to put art at the center of a just and democratic society. What would be the equivalent, in filmic terms, of a William Morris lecture? The task is daunting, especially since Morris spoke to audiences of the converted—or at least half-converted—to his ideas. But at least the dialectic of his lectures—the give and take of ideas—could be scripted into dialogue. His tone, while firm, is not dogmatic. Morris may be in his pulpit, and he may speak like a prophet, but there is also genuine humility in his stance and a profound awareness of how vulnerable art—for all its power—remains in a money economy. At almost every junction in his argument, he considers the objections to his ideas and acknowledges that the world is a long way from even approaching his view of the nexus between society and art. Certainly Morris's gentleness and extraordinary patience in the exposition of his ideas is an important supplement to Craigie's other great master, George Bernard Shaw, whose bluff, confident, prose in *The Intelligent Woman's Guide to* Socialism bowls the reader over. Although Shaw enjoins the intelligent woman to act on her own ideas, what intelligent woman—or man—can compete with Shaw's seething brain? Acting à la Shaw requires the kind of spark he plugs into Vivie, the "new woman" in *Mrs. Warren's Profession*. It is hard to imagine Shaw slowing down long enough to write a somber, measured Morris paragraph:

> But I think there will be others of you in whom vague discontent is stirring; who are oppressed by the life that surrounds you; confused and troubled by that oppression, and not knowing on which side to seek a remedy, though you are fain to do so: well, we, who have gone further into those troubles, believe that we can help you: true we cannot at once take your trouble from you; nay, we may at first rather add to it; but we can tell you what we think of the way out of it; and then amidst the many things you will have to do to set yourselves and others fairly on that way, you will many days, nay most days, forget your trouble in thinking of the good that lies beyond it, for which you are working.

Morris lacked one crucial element, humor, Craigie used to say. Shaw had humor, of course, but for the exuberant play of ideas about art, she took as her master Oscar Wilde (1854-1900).

"The Critic as Artist" establishes a style and a dialectic of ideas which not only inform Craigie's first documentary but which pervade her aesthetic for the rest of her life. "What is the use of art-criticism?" Ernest asks Gilbert, his interlocutor in Wilde's most famous essay. "Why can't the artist be left alone…Why should those who cannot create take upon themselves to estimate the value of creative work?" Gilbert's answer is that criticism is creative, that criticism in fact remakes works of art in the critic's imagination, and this process of creation and criticism go hand in hand and has done so since the time of the Greeks. In effect, Wilde (who weights the argument in Gilbert's favor) is suggesting that critics have to take possession of art and filter it through their sensibilities just as the artist first filtered it through his own. In other words, art cannot exist without criticism:

> I assure you, my dear Ernest, that the Greeks chattered about painters quite as much as people do nowadays, and had their private views, and shilling exhibitions and Arts and Crafts guilds, and Pre-Raphaelite movements, and movements toward realism, and lectured about art, and wrote essays on art, and produced their art-historians, and their archaeologists, and all the rest of it.

The experience of art, in fact, is a dialogue—as Craigie would presently dramatize in *Out of Chaos*—with an art critic occupying the center of her film.

Like Morris, Wilde dissolves distinctions: "To know the principle of the highest art is to know the principles of all the arts." Rejecting the Romantic view that art is inspiration, a welling up of thought and emotion, Gilbert counters: "Without the critical faculty, there is no artistic creation at all…All fine imaginative work is self-conscious and deliberate." To make this point in a documentary, Craigie realized, meant showing the artists at work and revealing the work of art as an unfolding, deliberative process. But, with one exception, it is not the artists who speak but the critic, for, as Gilbert remarks: "criticism demands infinitely more cultivation than creation does."

Like Morris's view of art, Wilde's is wrapped up in his conception of form. The critic shapes the work of art just as the artist shapes the world into the work of art: "The critic occupies the same relation to the work of art that he criticizes as the artist does to the visible world of form and colour, or the unseen world of passion and of thought." Put more simply and on a democratic level, Gilbert asserts that the "meaning of any beautiful created thing is, at least, as much in the soul of the him who looks at it, as it was in his soul who wrought it."

At an even more elementary level, Wilde explains why art is so necessary: "Life is terribly deficient in form." In other words, it is the artist's mandate to extricate form out of chaos—all the more so, of course, in wartime London. At no other point in modern history, Craigie realized, did the search for form suddenly become a vital, everyday concern. But her mission included not simply acknowledging art's newfound status but to argue, in her words, that the artist "should be part of everyday life more than a doctor or a lawyer." She made this point even clearer in Alan Reeve's *Picture Post* article announcing the release of *Out of Chaos*:

> With mass production, industrial design and town planning, the artist is becoming increasingly important and useful to society. He has been

neglected too long, and we can't live full lives if we continue to ignore him. If we question the look of a painting, we will also question the look of other things, our houses and our towns.

Without Craigie's sense of urgency, it is doubtful that *Out of Chaos* could have been made. It may seem, in retrospect, inevitable that someone would have made a film like hers during the war. At the time, however, no one, except Jill Craigie, had the idea for this film. Even in retrospect, the singularity of her work has been neglected. Only the *Picture Post* article recognized its originality and ambition—calling it "the first serious effort…to guide the public's wartime interest in art into something which may be permanent."

An independent director or producer—or anyone, really—who knows anything about the making of a film will wonder how a thirty-two-year old woman, in 1943, in the midst of a war, got the funding, assembled a crew, found the artists, and a company willing to distribute a documentary lasting a little less than thirty minutes. Even though the war did open up certain opportunities for women, the studios, the British Council, and the Ministry of Information did not suddenly employ a cadre of women directors. Craigie gave various, incomplete explanations of how she got to do the film. She said she went to J. Arthur Rank, the movie mogul, and convinced him of the film's timeliness. She said she had the good fortune to work for a remarkably generous producer, Filippo Del Giudice. She said she pitched her idea to Kenneth Clark, who surprisingly put his faith in this neophyte director. All true, but how did Craigie make these contacts? Where does the story begin?

During the making of *The Flemish Farm*, the film Craigie wrote with Jeffrey Dell, her second husband, William MacQuitty, their associate producer, used to drive over to Hampstead to pick up Jeffrey Dell, who had been asked to direct the film by Sidney Box. That is how MacQuitty met Craigie, an ardent woman, who used her big eyes, he remembered, to charm men. MacQuitty saw nothing amiss between husband and wife, although he noted that they had a sort of friendly rivalry as writers. Jill watched a jolly Jeffrey depart for the studio each day, and she became, MacQuitty suggests, jealous. She wanted to write and *direct*, and to MacQuitty she confided her idea of making a film about art and wartime artists.

Craigie could not have chosen a more receptive, perspicacious producer. William MacQuitty's life was—no hyperbole intended—a life to remember, the title of his superbly entertaining and inspiring autobiography. Born in 1905 in Belfast, he watched the launching of the Titanic and produced the classic film about its sinking, *A Night To Remember* in 1958. By the time he met Craigie, he had already spent fifteen years in the Far East with the Chartered Bank of India, pursued an adventurous love life, studied Eastern philosophy, and psychology under the tutelage of Wilhelm Stekel, one of Freud's original group who had broken off to develop his own brand of analysis—relying, as MacQuitty writes in *Life to Remember* on "using intuition to slip past the patient's resistance to being freed or cured." Stekel told MacQuitty that there is no suitable training for a psychoanalyst: "Either you are born a psychologist or you will never become one." MacQuitty qualified by birth, possessing as well an extraordinary eye, training himself as an exceptional photographer who would go on to publish collections of photographs on Persia, China, India, the great gardens of the world and establish The MacQuitty International Photographic Collection covering "aspects of life in over 70 countries" in more than a quarter of a million photographs dating from the 1920s to the present day. He broke into the film business the only way a MacQuitty can. Rather than seeking out John Grierson, universally recognized then as the impresario of documentary film, MacQuitty simply started his own company. Or as he said: "I paddle my own canoe."

MacQuitty took Craigie's idea to Sydney Box (1907-1983), a producer almost as remarkable as MacQuitty. "He had this effortless confidence, beyond belief," MacQuitty recalled. By the age of fourteen, Box became a sportswriter for a local newspaper in Beckenham, Kent. By eighteen he had written several one act plays and had produced a six-hour version of Ibsen's *Peer Gynt.* Like MacQuitty, this entrepreneur had established his own documentary film company, Verity Films, by the autumn of 1940. By 1943, it had become the largest producer of documentary films in the country, working in conjunction with both the Ministry of Information and the studios. A busy man who had as many as ten film units working simultaneously, Box promised MacQuitty that he would find a way to fit Craigie's film into his prodigious schedule. Like MacQuitty, Box did not discount women's talents. Indeed, his sister Betty got the job of supervising film units, "some of which were comprised of women directors and camera operators. (The war thus helped make at least a tiny dent in the traditional chauvinism of the film industry)," writes film historian Geoffrey Macnab in *J. Arthur Rank and the British Film Industry.*

To fund Craigie's documentary, Box worked through Filippo Del Giudice (1892-1961), senior producer for J. Arthur Rank (1888-1972), then at the height of his power in British films. Del, an extravagant Italian (exiled from fascist Italy), eagerly encouraged "ze new tal-ents"—as Craigie would say, mimicking his tendency to divide English words in two. He also "liked women," Craigie told

Charles Drazin. He had a mistress, the actress Greta Gynt, but his sexual adventures covered considerable ground—much more than any other producer Drazin investigated for his book on British cinema in the 1940s: "No one else I have written about in this book has been remembered with quite so much admiration and affection, nor with so many warnings of 'For God's sake, don't use this story!'" Craigie did not say to Drazin how involved she became personally with Del, but it is hard to imagine him not making a pass, to say the least.

Both MacQuitty and Box knew that they only had to sell Del on the idea of the film, and then Craigie could do what she wanted under the imprimatur of Del's company "Two Cities" (London and Rome). Del never seemed to visit a set while in production; he never interfered with directors or writers or the producers he engaged to work for him, saying "We all know that if you have a very good Director it is useless to interfere with his work…If you interfered it would be like looking over the shoulder of Picasso or Augustus John whilst they are doing their work. Anybody really great could not stand being watched in such a way." Although Del earned good money and critical acclaim for J. Arthur Rank with films such as Laurence Olivier's *Henry V*, he also spent it lavishly on himself and on his film projects. In this case, however, the sharper MacQuitty and Box figured out that the film could be done on location (thus taking up only a week of precious studio time and space) and for the modest sum of seven thousand pounds. Nevertheless, as MacQuitty points out: "Del was taking a risk with an untried woman director (women directors then being almost unheard-of) and a subject that lacked mass appeal. The British Council and the Arts Council, from whom we hoped for more backing, both turned the project down." As Laurence Olivier later said about Del: "I know no one else in British films so kind, generous, imaginative and courageous." Olivier's valedictory is not merely an expression of gratitude; it is a lament for a dream of film that dwindled after the war years and along with it the career of Jill Craigie. She acknowledged that Del "lived fairly extravagantly, not nearly as extravagantly as rich people live these days [1994] I may say, but he never feathered his nest, he wasn't in on the royalties; he didn't have control over the negatives, all these things that Alexander Korda always took control of, so he really was a patron of the arts, he did see himself as a kind of impresario."

Through Del, Craigie had access to J. Arthur Rank, who entered the British film industry in the mid 1930s and infused it with new life just as the initial successes of Korda and Co. were rapidly reversed in the late 1930s slump. Unlike many movie tycoons, Rank did not claim to know anything about making motion pictures. He could be remarkably generous in giving producers and directors the freedom to develop their projects without studio interference. On the other hand, as a businessman he sought control over finances and budgets through his notoriously mean accountant, John Davis (1906-1993). Rank's father had amassed his fortune in the flour milling business, and his just as successful son wanted to expand the family's fortune and spread its Methodist precepts by creating profit-making pictures with uplifting ideas and sound moral messages. You cannot spread the word if you do not have the funding for it, but the blessing of the funding derives, of course, from spreading the word. So any film with moral or idealistic pretensions would appeal to Rank but would also be chargeable to Davis's box office/entertainment value ledger. Films like Craigie's, in other words, incited wars over J. Arthur Rank's soul. The timing of her film, in the realm of Rank, proved propitious because at this stage Del's gains overcame his losses, and Rank's "evangelical side," notes film historian Geoffrey Macnab, "warmed to the Italian." Or as Craigie liked to say, "there was methodism in his madness."

Craigie also called Rank a "benevolent dictator," and that is why she went to him, she said, and put this idea: "Would you consider replacing the second feature film with British documentaries on things of social importance, in view of the war situation." The second feature was often a "quota quickie," a film produced mainly to fill the quota of British films mandated by a law aimed at reducing the overwhelming presence of the Hollywood product in British theatres. Since the second feature amounted to an add-on audiences tolerated, and because of the low entertainment expectations, Rank could afford to soothe his conscience without risking very much of his money. This was probably one of the few times Craigie actually spoke with Rank. "I'm a very small cog in this," Craigie told film historian Charles Drazin, "don't build me up as something too big, because I'm very small!"

Unlike the principal documentary filmmakers of her period who relied on government funding or were employed by private companies to make films for nontheatrical venues, Craigie had to deal with very negative market conditions. That Del proved susceptible to her ideas made her career possible, but his isolation as a producer ultimately contributed to her undoing. As Drazin points out, Del was "routinely ridiculed. His attempts to be innovative were dismissed in the trade magazines as fantastic nonsense. He was laughed at not because he was impractical but because he was trying to give exhibitors what in the main they did want: Art." This view of a film industry crunched in the vice of distributors and exhibitors is, in part, derived from Drazin's probing interview with Craigie while preparing his study, *The Finest Years: British Cinema of the 1940s*. Film historians, except for Drazin and Macnab, have ignored that she overcame so much obstructiveness with style and aplomb in the next three years. Thus Ernest Betts writes: "scarcely any individual succeeded notably in the documentary film outside the co-operative and outside the documentary's relationship with public purposes and finance deriving from it." Such a sentence can be left standing only by virtue of its escape clause ("scarcely") or defended by denying that Jill Craigie "succeeded notably"—which, for all her films' faults, is not a tenable proposition.

In *A Life to Remember*, MacQuitty pinpoints Craigie's irresistible blend of beauty and pluck:

> Jill was small, dark, pretty and determined—very determined. Her script was to answer those questions that arose in the minds of the public when they saw their money being spent on artists whose work they regarded with suspicion or ridicule.

In a later interview, he described her as "eager," which captured the infectious quality of her drive—especially appealing to men because she was so compactly yet sturdily put together. There seemed nothing extravagant about her pitching a project that entailed considerable cooperation from important figures in the art world. MacQuitty and Craigie's accounts agree that the pivotal personality in their enterprise was Kenneth Clark. As she remembered it:

> I went to Kenneth Clark and I said: I want to make a film about the war artists. I want to put them on the screen, and you too, and I'm very keen on certain artists, which I told him, and that won his approval. "I know nothing about films," I said, "but I'm sure I can manage somehow. Well of course I was trying to talk before, you know, before I knew anything. However, I got his backing.

Confident, but not arrogant, certain about her art, uncertain about her film work, but also offering him the opportunity to shape the public's perception of art—altogether she put on a well-balanced and appealing performance. Of course, her memory of that scene with Clark could be faulty; telling the story after the event is always a license for embroidery and selectivity. However, the tenor of MacQuitty's recollections reinforce her own.

What did Clark make of this enticing amalgam of hubris and humility? MacQuitty said she had "enormous feminine charm and original ideas." He found her rather refreshing to work with, a relief from the tetchy egos of male directors. "She was wonderful with people." She had to be, for she was quite aware, as she said decades later, that her virtually all male crew that eventually numbered forty initially looked at her as no more than a "girl." "She was able to stroke the male ego with enormous effect," MacQuitty said. A female interviewer once pressed Craigie on this subject:

> [Interviewer] You did tell me once that you weren't above using the fact that you were a woman for getting a film underway.
> [Craigie] I think that when women enter public life of any sort...they should not lose their charm. I am conscious of the fact that when there are debates in the House of Commons about women voting...the anti-suffragettes frequently say this...repeat it over and over "Women will lose their charm and will become aggressive." Well, men don't...lose their charm. But women...sometimes become—the politicians—too aggressive, a bit too tub-thumping, and remembering all these things that I had read, I was not above exercising an occasional womanly wile.
> [Interviewer] In what way?
> [Craigie] Well—I might flatter a fellow perhaps to get a film going. I might say..."If you don't do it, nobody else will." Which was true, incidentally. I tried not to get into fierce argument, or pour scorn on...a man who said to me, "Why do you do this?" or "Why don't you do this?" and though it was the most ghastly idea I had ever heard, I would never let him know. I'd say, "Well, that's a marvellous idea, BUT"...and find some way round it. It was very difficult to be absolutely straightforward then, I think, if you wanted to do something, if you had a sufficient passion to. I really had a passion to translate my visions into actions and so I was prepared to—not go very far, mind you, don't get the wrong idea, but I did what I could to get my own way.

The circumspect MacQuitty ventured only the comment that "I imagine most men found her attractive. But that did not mean they got anywhere." Of his own relationship with Craigie he commented: "I was the other half," meaning she did the writing and directing, and he engaged the cameraman and crew and dealt with the other mechanics and business of filmmaking.

Unfortunately, Clark does not mention Craigie or her film in his autobiography, Meryle Secrest, *Kenneth Clark: A Biography* (1984), does not plug this gap. But Craigie's boldness is evident, for as Clark does say in *The Other Half: A Self-Portrait*: "at that date films and film-makers were suspect." Shoddy newsreel companies, the extravagances of Korda and others, put off people who took their art seriously. Fortunately for Craigie, Clark's experience as head of the film division at the Ministry of Information had been positive, and he considered certain film industry leaders such as Michael Balcon and Sidney Bernstein "remarkable men, intelligent, easy to deal with, and, for the most part, public-spirited." He also may have been impressed with Craigie's partiality to Henry Moore's tube shelter drawings, which Clark calls in *The Other Half* the "greatest works of art inspired by the war."

According to Craigie, Clark gave her full backing but "left it to me to persuade the war artists to appear in the film." Of those she had in mind, only John Piper refused. "And rightly so," Craigie added, "I was not only young and naïve, but had no experience in directing a film." Alan Reeve, author of a feature article on the film published before its release reports that Craigie had to "overcome the nervousness and suspicion of the artists, none of who were anxious to star in the movies. But once having gained faith in her as a sympathetic director, they responded intelligently." Craigie, on the other hand, remembered that the artists "seemed most eager to be filmed and only wanted to know when, where and how." And MacQuitty remembered: "It was a time of heightened adrenalin. All the artists were totally dedicated to capturing their response to war and showing what it felt like to be in a country that was at war. They all drew upon their deepest reserves."

MacQuitty recalled that he and Craigie first set out with cameraman Pennington "Penny" Richards, and a loader-clapper boy, Leslie Hughes, to film Paul Nash (1889-1946), then a renowned artist in the tradition of Blake and Turner who identified himself by the mid-1930s with the surrealists. Primarily a landscape painter, Nash had produced extraordinary images of a devastated countryside in the First World War. In the Second World War, he produced his masterpiece, *Totes Meer* (*Dead Sea* 1940-1941, now at the Tate), a symbolic—almost allegorical—vision of a landscape strewn with shot-down German and British planes—waves and waves of them with their wings overlapping in a concentrated complex of bent metal that evoked the German onrush of bombers over Britain and the aftermath of the country's heroic defense. MacQuitty vividly describes the scene shot for the film: "Engines had smashed through air-frames already riddled with bullets and grotesquely melted seats nestled in the wreckage so that you half expected to see human fragments amid the horror." The artist guided them through the ghastly site. A fine photographer, Nash took an interest in Penny's light-meter while an impatient Craigie kept urging the cameraman to shoot. But Penny was waiting for consistent lighting so that he could film a whole sequence. New to the technicalities of filmmaking, Craigie said to Penny, "I can't see any difference." Paul Nash, "an impressive, withdrawn man with penetrating eyes and wit," took an admiring look at Craigie and said, "Not even with those beautiful eyes."

Craigie's memory of Nash reveals how crucial MacQuitty became to the conception of her work and how critical she could be of her own pretensions:

> He [MacQuitty] really had quite crude ideas about art, then. And I was really rather priggish. I used to say, "Don't say I know what I like, you know, the artist won't like it if you say that…. I used to give him these hints. However, we were in the National Gallery and we were looking at Nash's painting and suddenly to my astonishment MacQuitty said: "Oh, the poor fellow. He's really suffering from claustrophobia. He needs air. I thought this was the most remarkable statement from someone who knew nothing about painting! I didn't know what he meant and why he said it. He was one of these Irishmen who'd been all over the world and done everything, you know…and he'd studied psychology for a while under Stekel. And he knew how to interpret dreams, and he could see from the surrealist themes that this fellow was gasping for air. Well then we went to Nash's home to film him, because I also took Liam—as I called him—to look at the paintings before we met the artist, it was all part of the game, and when we went to his home he was in a tiny little room. His wife was an Egyptologist, and the kitchen table was filled with rubbish and debris and brushes and combs and washing-up brushes, a complete muddle and a tiny little space was left for Paul to have his lunch. You could see immediately that the whole thing was on top of him, which was why he was gasping to get out…. After that Mac-Quitty himself took a much more sophisticated interest in painting, and then acquired a wonderful collection. He became a great connoisseur in no time…. I was a little prig thinking I knew everything and he knew nothing, but he knew more than me, really.

Craigie neglects one detail that MacQuitty includes in *A Life to Remember*. Nash suffered from asthma and stopped often to use his inhaler as he guided them through the plane wreckage.

In her *Out of Chaos* scrapbook, Craigie recalls how obsessed Nash became by the "strange shapes made by smashed aeroplanes. We spent much time on the aeroplane dump which was *huge*, seemed to stretch for miles." She found an emotional element lacking in Nash's paintings, which he should have given a "more sinister quality."

Craigie and her crew then shot Graham Sutherland (1903-1980) at the Imperial Chemical Limestone Quarries at Hindlow, Buxton. The artist had come into his own in the 1930s in a series of oil paintings that depicted landscapes of "semi-abstract patterns of haunting and monstrous shapes," almost as if he had been anticipating a holocaust. Craigie liked to tell the story, Michael Foot, her third husband, remembered, about photographing Sutherland doing an

> odd sketch every now and again. He scuppers it out because he doesn't think it is any good. And he throws it out on the pavement as he is going by. Liam MacQuitty picks it up and stretches it out, and Graham Sutherland says, "That's fifteen quid it will cost you."

MacQuitty remembered Sutherland as "dapper and forceful"; Craigie called him "rather vain." He wanted to be filmed wearing a helmet (he was) and "doing important things." and "involved in the war," she confided in her scrapbook, where she also recalled that she had tried to film Sutherland drawing in a Cornish tin mine. But the conditions proved too daunting, and she watched in dismay as he tore up his "marvellous" pictures. She did not get on with him that well, although they shared a devotion to socialist politics. He was "so taken" with MacQuitty that Craigie suspected "homosexuality. When signing a hotel form, elaborate documents during the war, he came to the blank line beside SEX. He looked at MacQuitty and said, 'I never know what to put for that.'"

Stanley Spencer (1891-1959), easily the most flamboyant artist to be filmed, is widely regarded as one of the most original figures in 20th-century British art. Like Paul Nash, he created distinguished works of art during both world wars, concentrating in the former on the lives of ordinary soldiers—as in *The Dug-Out*—and on war workers in the latter, focusing on shipbuilders on the Clyde. Spencer was so spectacularly odd that Craigie chided biographer Fiona McCarthy in a book review: "She even denies that he was eccentric." Craigie contended the artist was "quite mad. She remembered traveling with him, third class in a train carriage, and announcing to the mothers and children "all my painting is masturbation. I masturbate, and masturbate, and masturbate." He did his sketches on toilet paper and would say, "My lavatory paper is worth more than your cameras." Craigie noted in her scrapbook: "Toilet paper not so soft or absorbent as it became after the war." She found him "always outrageous. "He liked dirt, and he wore dirty pajamas, and he smelled quite badly. He approved of dirt for its own sake." Such comments, however, reflect amusement, not disapproval. Malcolm Macdonald, one of Spencer's patrons, derived enormous amusement when commissionaires would not allow scruffy, smelly Stanley to join his host until Malcolm vouched for him. At some meals the scatological Spencer talked nonsense; at other others he seemed the "cleverest of us all" and a "genius," Craigie remembered. She walked with him on Hampstead Heath, and he would stoop to study dog droppings with infinite care. Looking a fine mess, Stanley would stand on Craigie's doorstep with arms outstretched and boom: "Why am I so attractive to women?" He complained of his female lovers, "They're all so big...And they knock me about." Craigie troubled herself to ask one of the artist's "big-boned" women, Daphne Charlton, about Stanley, and Daphne admitted that she did "knock Stanley about occasionally." He could be "so infuriating." In *A Life to Remember*, MacQuitty wrote that Stanley, just before boarding a train, said to him: "You mustn't let Daphne come with us. She is stronger than I am and every afternoon when I was painting in Exeter she would carry me off to bed." It was a "near thing," MacQuitty remembered, "but we waved her goodbye." What did women see in Stanley, Craigie wondered, and concluded they fell in love with his art.

Craigie's film captures the extraordinary intensity and joy Spencer took in his work. Indeed, of all the artists in *Out of Chaos*, he exudes the idea of the worker—not because of the way he is dressed or because of what he is doing but because of his air of preoccupation with his task. He seems at one with the shipyard environment. As Fiona McCarthy observes, the "lives of ordinary working people interested him immensely." Another Spencer biographer reports that "he lived entirely among the shipyard people," who had no idea he was a famous artist—in part because he did not seek out prominent or educated figures. William Morris's spirit breathes in Spencer's paintings of shipbuilders and in his statement about the men and equipment he depicted: "Everything I see is manifestly religious and sexual...it is not that coils of rope suggest haloes it is just that all these men, hawsers, strings, as in all forms have a hallowing effect of their own...it is part of their nature." There is the Morris touch: "as in all forms." An epic, mural like quality suffuses Spencer's panoramic painting of the shipbuilding process. The horizontal elongation of the canvas jammed with an extraordinary range of individual and collective activity suggests the elemental, Meso-American look of Diego Rivera's murals of the automobile workers housed in the Detroit Institute of Arts. But the film focused not so much on the finished product as on Stanley in situ: "In my work I am exposed far more to the weather than a great many people whether soldiers or sailors or any of the civil defence services. I have to rough it, I can tell you." He spent much of his time drenched in water, wading in water, and wet from top to toe. The film does not contain his statement, but it does capture the way Spencer *exposed* himself to the conditions of his worker-subjects more powerfully than his own self-serving statement does. Watching Spencer excitedly drawing the workers' different positions and attitudes reified Craigie's "socialist beliefs. Workers had bad teeth & were of stunted growth," she scrawled in her scrapbook next to a photograph of Stanley absorbed in appraising one of his drawings. MacQuitty remembers that the artist was "immensely popular" among the shipbuilders. Watching Stanley sketch in "rapid bursts on a roll of strong white toilet paper" made MacQuitty think of "papyrus scrolls of ancient scribes." MacQuitty asked him why he used toilet paper. "Because it is cheap and doesn't end. It gives me continuity, and if I don't like the sketch I don't have to waste the paper!" Spencer grinned. "Stanley was very appealing," MacQuitty said.

Yet the star in Craigie's film and in her memory of making it remained Henry Moore (1898-1986). Like the other artists in *Out of Chaos*, he had a considerable reputation among his fellow artists and the critics but was not yet the world figure he would become after the war. The son of a Yorkshire miner, Moore had a tactile and earthy sensibility that made his work—in stone or wood—sensuous and palpable. His abstractions of the human figure contain a "vital force and vigour" that derived from his absorption in the swelling, rhythmic bodies in the frescoes of Masaccio (1401-1428), one of the key figures of the Renaissance, and from the pent-up energy and monumental presence of the human form in Meso-American and Sumerian sculpture. Recalling Moore's reputation before the war, Craigie later said, "His curious sculptures with their famous holes could enrage even some well-known collectors of Post-Impressionists."

Craigie took her crew, now numbering forty technicians, to film Moore in the Hampstead tube station, where he made his famous drawings of the shelterers and to his studio. "They expected they might encounter a weird fellow talking about art in incomprehensible language," Craigie wrote in her memoir of filming Moore. They soon thought differently of this "down-to-earth" Yorkshireman. "He alone spent hours with me in advance to ensure that I had the right ideas. A more engaging teacher it would have been impossible to find." In fact, Moore had been a teacher of art, and he paid Craigie and her crew the sublime William Morris compliment of treating them as fellow artists.

Henry and Jill walked together hand-in-hand in the underground tube/tomb. They shared what Moore called a "morbid curiosity & a strange, subdued excitement," observing the scene that had stirred some of his greatest art: the sight of a sea of figures swaddled together, rolling over and pitching against each other, slumbering in exhausted, fitful sleep, and collapsing into stillness—in the dim light looking to Craigie like "rows of Egyptian mummies." Moore watched, making notes and brief sketches, catching the anxiety just behind the "bonhomie" of these plucky people. "He could hardly suppress his anger at what was happening to these people," Craigie remembered. "Two women restlessly asleep clutched at their blankets as if they were both in the grip of a nightmare. He proposed to recreate this impression for the benefit of our film."

Moore was the only artist who discussed with Craigie the nature of film as an artistic medium:

> He had already told me that he considered the reclining figure most appropriate to the hard, heavy qualities of stone and bronze, more true to the materials than portrayals of actions, such as running or wrestling. That being so, I asked him whether he agreed that to be true to the medium of cinematic film, movies should move. "Of course," he replied, as if he had already given some thought to the matter.

Film would become, in Moore's hands, another way of presenting his portfolio. Although *Picture Post* did a feature on the film while it was still in production, and *Out of Chaos* received the kind of publicity accorded feature films, other than Craigie, only Lee Miller, the renowned photographer, and her journalist colleague from *Life* magazine, recognized the significance of shooting Moore at work.

In Moore's studio, the army of technicians trampled about examining Moore's work, and Craigie observed their puzzled faces, imagining them trying to

> reconcile so much rubbish with so commonsensical a man. They were in for a big surprise. We focused the camera on a blank sheet of white paper and called for action. Henry then took a white wax crayon and seemed to scribble all over it. As the white upon white was invisible he appeared to have no way of seeing precisely what he was doing. He gave the impression he might just as well have been blindfolded. He then washed the paper all over with a brush filled with a dark water-colour. Naturally the water could not take on the wax, the colour could only fill in the spaces left by the artist. Magically, a powerful impression of two women restlessly asleep in the Underground appeared, the whole creating an atmosphere of oppression beyond the scope of a photograph. The execution of the work was so beautifully timed and adapted to a medium devised for action—it was shot in one take—that Henry's conquest of the film unit was complete.

During a break in filming Craigie asked him about his interest in three-dimensional form. He explained that he used to ease the pain of his mother's lumbago: "He demonstrated the movement first by rubbing his own hip, then mine. To have Henry Moore rub one's hip is not an experience anyone would be likely to forget. To rub one's hand over a Moore sculpture, which he liked people to do, is often reminiscent of stroking a hip." But why the small heads and holes? she asked. He replied that these elements evoke an aura of dignity and mystery.

Craigie's memoir of working with Moore is of a piece with her film. Writing forty-three years after the release of *Out of Chaos*, Craigie echoed the words of Eric Newton, the critic in her film: "as with most of the greatest artists and composers, [Moore's] work was widely denounced until it became more familiar. People do not know what they like so much as like what they know." Moore taught Craigie and her crew something new and fresh and creative to like, and he did so through understanding the terms and conditions of film work:

> He made only one request; the filming of his sculpture must be left to the last. Lighting interiors was then more complicated than it is today, requiring many more lamps, each with it own name, complete with gauzes and other paraphernalia. When the lighting cameraman gave instructions to a team of electricians, he used technical terms beyond the comprehension of laymen. When the time came, Henry took the cameraman aside and quietly told him just how to light the sculpture not merely by suggesting where a shadow should fall and whether the correct depth of shade had been achieved, but by using all the right technical terms.

Everyone left the studio certain of Moore's genius. Although Craigie gives all the credit to Moore, he obviously responded to a sensitive and perceptive filmmaker who created the conditions in which he could educate and edify his audience.

MacQuitty's memory of filming Moore meshes with Craigie's, especially his observation of a "strong, quiet man with a simple, natural way of explaining what he was doing." Similarly, magazine editor Tom Hopkinson who frequently lunched with Moore during this period, noted: "I had never met anyone so calm, so certain of himself and of what he was doing, and so generous towards the work of everybody else." Although Moore did many of his sketches in the Hampstead tube station, MacQuitty remembers that for the film scenes were shot in Holborn. He also mentions Moore's "charming wife," Irina, whom Craigie liked very much—so much that she resisted the very powerful temptation to act on her erotic attraction to the artist. To the end of her life, she was both proud that she had respected his marriage and regretful that she had not made love to Moore. Craigie kept photographs of herself, Henry, Irina, and Lee Miller seated around a table and clearly enjoying each other's company.

Out of Chaos begins with a portentous trumpet solo of single, deliberately stated notes soon joined by the London Symphony orchestra which mimics and amplifies the trumpet fanfare adding strings and percussion and then more brass, with this theme repeated during a shot of what looks like cave drawings of animals and a human figure, followed by a script superimposed on the graphic, acknowledging the compulsion to create art and a recognition of the individual/communal dialogue that makes the artist a central yet problematic figure in civilization:

> Soon after man learned to walk on two legs he wanted to draw. At first he drew on the wall of his cave, and no doubt when his neighbours saw what he'd done, they argued about it. The kind of argument they had has gone on ever since.

The intricacy of this opening, the fusing of sound and image, so familiar as to be taken for granted in later documentaries, was a new element Craigie worked perhaps a little too strenuously to establish, wishing to catch the attention of theatregoers, most of whom would not be interested in art per se but who might be captivated if art could be melded to the visual and aural medium of film. The call and response of single instrument and orchestra, which evokes the natural, inevitable, contrapuntal dynamic of creation and criticism, is the beginning of a fugue-like structure which the film's composer, Lennox Berkeley, called "setting a painting to music as one might set a poem." He keyed his music to the three-part presentation of each major artist: 1. The musical impression of the scene the artist painted. 2. An elaboration of that impression while showing the artist at work. 3. A "more orderly construction" of impression and elaboration to accompany the present of the artist's completed work.

The concatenation of the opening words and music is followed by shots of people entering the National Gallery on a Saturday afternoon. An unidentified voice of a young sounding female narrator (it could be Craigie) notes that attendance during the war is "different." Who are these people? Part of an "arty minority?" Men and women in uniform are shown gazing at paintings. "Do they often come here?" the narrator asks. A shot of a studious young man in glasses prompts the narrator to say he is the type you would expect to find in a gallery. Three men with their backs turned to the camera suggest a group of businessman.

The well-tried technique of the voice-over narrator is freshened by this conceit of an observer in the room intimately speaking to us and asking why during a world war all these different kinds of people exhibit "this terrific interest in painting?"

The tone is casual, but the film's didactic purpose is evident and perhaps patronizing, though mildly so as the narrator swiftly provides a potted history of what led to this gathering in the gallery. The narrator recalls how artists, housewives, and institutions of various kinds "packed up" their treasures in anticipation of attack. The muted trumpet solo and the orchestra underscore this sense of going underground and hiding. With a war on, the narrator notes, there was not much interest in art. The camera and the narrator then segue to an establishing shot of Kenneth Clark, director of the National Gallery, who, the narrator reports, suggested artists be employed to record the war, and got government backing for his scheme. Clark sits at a desk and begins giving the history of his effort as if he has just heard the narrator introduce him. He is stiff and looks down (evidently reading from a script). He then rises and perches on the corner of the desk and looks down at the paper on it. He moves his hands uncomfortably on the desk. With an astonishing lack of perception and paucity of research, Meryle Secrest refers to his "aplomb," as though this is the same personality who enlivened his justly renowned Civilization series in the 1970s. In 1943, Clark had no idea how to appear in front of a camera; nor did most men in his position, and part of the awkwardness *Out of Chaos* is due to a cast that had no experience in the medium or any feel for it. Clark learned, like others a whole generation later, how to "be themselves" in front of a camera, but there was no way Craigie could endow him with that experience beforehand. MacQuitty remembered Clark's nervousness, and that Craigie suggested he sit on the edge of his desk (movement does alleviate his awkwardness). At least one close-up might have made Clark seem less remote, but the brief medium shot (with sculpture in the background) just emphasizes his position of authority. MacQuitty photographed Clark and asked him for an autograph. "From your most incompetent and overpaid stand-in," Clark wrote. In her scrapbook, Craigie only remembered how eager and helpful he remained throughout the filming.

Mercifully after a minute or so the camera cuts to scenes with the artists out in the field, so to speak, sketching men at war with Clark's voice over explanation of the artists' activities. But then the camera returns to Clark walking about his office showing examples of war art—paintings of aircraft production and land girls, before shifting again to a shot of Stanley Spencer walking toward the camera, squinting and holding a sketchbook at the Clyde shipbuilding works. Multiple shots show Stanley observing workers crouching and stretching and bending as they weld and hammer machinery. He stands drawing the ribs of ships and girders. "The men in the shipyards seem to enjoy seeing themselves from a new point of view," the narrator notes as we see a shot of him unrolling his toilet paper for them to look at.

Shifting from scenes of Spencer watching the workers, to close-ups of his solitary work in his studio, and finally to a shot which closes in on one of Spencer's narrow horizontal scenes capturing the entire process of shipbuilding, the narrator concludes: "Some of us can interpret these compositions for ourselves, but it is usually a help to hear what a perceptive critic like Eric Newton has to say about them." Newton's voice over interpretation, unfortunately, emphasizes only the somber aspects of Spencer's vision: "Human beings toiling fantastically in a world of steel like lost souls in a medieval last judgment are caught up in a complex machine, but it is a machine of their own devising, smooth, polished, and irreligious." As the camera tracks across the painting emphasizing its elongated horizontality and the music takes on a brooding, less declarative tone, Newton emphasizes how carefully and repeatedly the artist has watched this scene until his art, like that of the workers, "turns the chaos of metal into a pattern and so intensifying its meaning."

This first sequence with Spencer takes no more than two minutes—an injection of art criticism immediately overtaken by images of planes in the sky and the narrator's newsreel change of tempo: "September 1940, the Battle of Britain, when so many of us were jolted out of our old way of living. And our old way of thinking." Scenes of downed planes with Nazi insignia shift to a medium shot of Paul Nash sketching the wreckage juxtaposed against a close-up of his prewar surrealistic landscapes. The camera then tracks from right to left (reversing the direction in which Spencer's painting was presented) and then diagonally downwards evoking the fall of these plane parts from the sky. The narrator explains that Nash wanted to make "images on the popular mind…encouraging to ourselves but depressing to the enemy." Focusing on his masterpiece which transforms the wreckage into a dead sea, the film superimposes a shot of the sea onto the painting and then ingeniously scrolls images of the same scene in different shades of light from dusk to twilight to reveal not only the different times at which Nash painted but also how this complex pattern of light is filtered into the painting's final composition. Surveying the scene, the narrator proceeds: "It seemed to him that the wreckage heaved itself up and down in a great tide flooding the fields," and then she defers again to Newton in voice-over describing the actual painting as a "picture of death with skeletons like the skeletons of prehistoric animals lying in a tangled mess." The heaving up of the metal reminds the critic of the "last agony of the German air fleet."

The narrator then recounts how fireman (shots appear from Humphrey Jennings's wartime classic *Fires Were Started*) felt called upon to paint the "astonishing scene they had taken part in." As several examples of the firemens' art are shown, the narrator notes that they also initiated an exhibition of their work seen all over the world which stimulated many who had never been to an art gallery to develop the habit of attending other shows. From this collective scene of fireman artists the film switches to a shot of perhaps the most remarkable of the group, Leonard Rosoman working at his canvas. Like so much of the film, this sequence moves forward and backward visually and aurally between groups and individuals and between orchestral backgrounds and solo notes.

The evocation of the fires provides a natural transition to scenes of Henry Moore walking among the shelterers in the underground. As Moore watches the "stoic endurance and suffering of these people," and the camera pans right to left across the bodies of sleepers, the narrator suggests he is the "one artist" most capable of "immortalizing" the scene. Then Moore is portrayed in his studio making one of his famous white crayon drawings. As he works on paper the camera provide close-ups of his miniature figures and focuses on the artist, the only one to speak in the film. With a calm and natural delivery, he describes how he uses the white crayon to capture the parts of the figure that are going to "catch the light.... It's more or less feeling the form without seeing it." He then shows how he uses a gray watercolor to cover the entire sheet of paper and then blots it with newspaper to complete just the first stage of the work. It's a magical yet unpretentious performance that deserves the word "aplomb."

In perfect Wildean mode, the narrator turns from the creator to the critic to analyze the finished product. Describing the picture of two people sleeping, Newton declares that

> Henry Moore has discovered the very rhythm of sleep. A great rolling movement runs across the drawing, like a broad Atlantic swell or like the rocking lilt of a lullaby. The rhythm is just but only just broken by the lines of the listless tired fingers. Deep shadows brood over the picture, and out of the shadows emerge two heads sunk in uneasy sleep. There are no sharp details—only the mouths and nostrils of the sleepers stand out in sharp relief, the slow breathing of exhaustion, an unnatural sleep troubled by memories of fear. It's an oasis of tranquility.

As these words are spoken images of actual sleepers briefly replace Moore's composition, reinforcing the nexus between the artist's observation and his imagination, between the people he observes and himself.

The Blitz brought the artist and the man in the street closer together, the narrator recapitulates, crediting artist Dennis Matthews with an organizing capacity that led to discovering an unused gallery in Bond Street, where the work of Civil Defense Artists was shown. Jill and Dennis had spent much time together in their ARP "battle headquarters…linked by phone to other areas and from where we could be called out to cope with casualties etc. of the Blitz," Craigie recalled in her scrapbook. In the film, shots of enthusiastic painters bringing in their work, and an up-tempo musical score introduce a brief speech by the Home Secretary predicting, "this bond between the artist and the man in the street will outlast the war." The narrator adds that all over the country such activities have inspired amateur and professional painters, and the Home Secretary's speech ends with his conviction that the artist is valuable for bringing color and imagination to everyday life.

Out of Chaos then comes full circle to the opening shots of the National Gallery to find out what people think about the art. Their opinions (which Craigie actually heard in galleries) are a compendium of typical responses to modern art.

> What interesting tone value.
> I can't explain what I mean, but I know what I like.
> I don't know what I like until I've worked it out.
> If this is painting, my small son's a genius.

"What would happen if they all got together?" the narrator asks. Gathered together around a painting they are disputing its merits, one commenting on the artist's reputation, another urging the others to "just look at it," another saying "people can't always see what they're looking at." One sees a rhythm in the painting; another does not. The debate continues, although one debater argues, "it's no use arguing about art." The narrator breaks in to say, "they will never get anywhere that way. We better get Eric Newton himself." Carrying himself in the Kenneth Clark school of stiffness, Newton appears on camera for the first time, striding with his hands behind his back and sounding like a schoolmaster: "What's all the trouble about?" He looks at the painting: "Oh, Graham Sutherland. Yes, it's pretty good." "Good!" says one outraged viewer, who does not believe Sutherland has ever seen a limestone quarry, the subject of the painting.

Perhaps only a consummate actor in a dialogue by Oscar Wilde could pull off this rather stagy scene. Newton's funereal face and his inability through gesture or manner to establish a rapport with the group dooms Craigie's effort to break down the divide between artist/critic and audience. Both director and critic understood the problem, but they could not surmount it. As Craigie said in her scrapbook: "He spoke about the joys of painting and the enjoyment to be had out of looking at painting while looking so gloomy that I felt he was having the opposite effect from the one intended. Could not get him to lighten his delivery."

The dialogue does a good job of explaining why paintings, like books, need to be read, and why the artist paints what nature cannot provide. It is all sound Wildean wisdom. Like the earlier sequences on the artists, the Sutherland segment juxtaposes the painting with the actual scenes he studied for his work and shows Sutherland with that much-coveted helmet on his head surveying the scene. Newton's voice over follows the artist observing men, shapes, landscape, and machinery in visually appealing progression. The artist stores up, simplifies, and makes sketches—"short hand notes"—that he takes back to his studio to shape the raw material into the finished work of art, Newton concludes. "Now he knows what he wants." Trying his best to smile, Newton is shown looking at one of the viewers and saying "very different from the real quarry, as prose is very different from poetry." Centering on the painting again, a shot removes the painting's dark sky to show "how all the drama is gone." Arrows point toward the swirling rhythm of the painting and the oppressiveness of nature that engulfs the pale quarry buildings. Everything by man in the painting is blocked out in white to show the clash between the man made geometrical forms and the curvilinear natural structures. This central idea is then compared to Sutherland's paintings of Cornish tin mines and the Blitz—thus cultivating an expanded sense of art that Wilde advocated as the critic's main task.

With this sense of art as a carefully worked-over process—a job of work as Wilde would have it, not a frill or inspiration of the moment—the film returns to its initial conception that art is an argument. One of the gallery spectators asks Newton whether Sutherland's art is "beautiful." He replies by suggesting that if we do not understand a work of art, we call it ugly and reserve the term beautiful for what we think we know. To the scoffer in his group, Newton points out that "you don't earn much of a living by pulling people's legs." When another notes that Turner and Constable do not need to be explained, Newton points out that in their time these artists were greeted with the same misunderstanding and bafflement as contemporary artists encounter. He cites one critic, for example, dismissing a Constable: "Did Mr. Constable ever see anything like this in nature?" But now, the critic emphasizes, these artists have taught us to see through their eyes. A reaction shot shows one of the most skeptical men in the group taking in for the first time a notion of art far greater than was dreamed of in his philosophy. But then in one remarkable touch—a true Jill Craigie socialist/democratic touch—a museum guard speaks to the critic:

> May I but in sir? An old lady in the gallery the other day looking at the Henry Moore's came to me and said "They're positively disgusting, an insult to the human form. If I had my way, I'd rip them out of their frames."

Newton, taking the comment in stride, treats it as an "old story" and a typical response to the new and adds: "Sooner or later everyone begins to suffer from a sort of hardening of the aesthetic arteries. It will happen to me one day. People say 'I know what I like." But they really mean 'I like what I know.'" Another skeptic still wonders, "What's the point of it all?" To simply increase the enjoyment of life, to learn to read in another way, the critic rejoins as the camera pans across several paintings and the narrator exhorts the audience to look at pictures "again and again." To keep looking is to begin to appreciate the art of painting, "which is part of the art of living," Against this varied display of paintings of common objects (a shoe), grand landscapes, voluptuous reclining nudes, and beach scenes, the full orchestra brings the film to a triumphal, resounding conclusion.

Although *Out of Chaos* cost the Rank organization only seven thousand pounds—not an enormous sum for a documentary in 1943—Rank's accountant, John Davis, who arranged for theatre bookings, did not think the money could be recouped. "Del and John Davis were at each other's throats," Craigie remembered, and Davis convinced Rank that her film was "absolute rubbish." Del did his best for Craigie, but he sent her a discouraging letter on 6 October 1944: "It would be a very good thing if the British Council were to buy the film. I do not think they can afford the money we have spent, but it is very difficult to get any substantial amount of money from the Exhibitors and this last point deters me from planning any production of shorts for the future." He sent Craigie into the studio for publicity shots and played up her role as a woman director in charge of a forty-man crew. (Craigie noted in her scrapbook that the only other woman on the production was the continuity girl). She disliked posing for the cameras and would be "quite scornful" in later years about the sepia glamour shots.

Reviewers, invited to private screenings, liked the film—with reservations. *The Times* (7 December 1944) was typical, noting that the film did not fit into "any obvious category." It represented not merely a portrayal of the artists but was itself a work of interpretation. The final paragraph still seems a fair summary judgment:

> *Out of Chaos* is not, in the event, quite as exciting a film as it promised to be. Its treatment of its most interesting subject is a shade too pedestrian and imitative of the orthodox documentary, but at least it is a film well worth making, and it is to be hoped that it will be widely shown.

Ernest Betts saw the film's historic importance, writing in the *Sunday Express* 10 December 1944):

> It tries something new and advances the cause of the cinema as an intelligent medium. It is so good. In fact, it isn't being shown anywhere! No release has been set, but it will be and the sooner the better.

Slowly, MacQuitty reports, the film made it into art houses, but "it received no general distribution and thus, after all the hard work, all the hopes and fears, all the wonderful notices, remained on the distributor's shelves." Even worse, according to Craigie, "they tore up the negative." But this was the "first film about modern art," she added, and "there were various prints around the place and people took negatives from the prints...and today if anybody wants any stuff about Henry Moore...they have to use the bit that I did in his studio, and they charge seven thousand pounds for it."

The Way We Live

As Craigie told a reporter doing a feature on *Out of Chaos*, she hoped to "tell the story of town planning in Britain [*The Way We Live*], and expose obstacles in the way of its enlightened achievement. Like many other documentary filmmakers, she was responding to the idea of a "better Britain. As Michael Foot so eloquently put it in his biography of Aneurin Bevan:

> Film producers began to recognize that the real life of the people was more exciting than bedroom farces in historical fancy dress. Publishers suddenly discovered that they could sell vast numbers of books on political and sociological topics.... Community life, so far from being disrupted by bombs and blackouts, was being richly renewed.... Men and women became true neighbours, even comrades, and England caught a glimpse of what a co-operative Commonwealth might be.

Craigie was reading Lewis Mumford on town planning and architecture: "I like to get one author and read everything that he's written on—usually it was 'he' then.... I read nearly all the books of the architects.... I was interested in the arts, and home-making, I suppose not having a home—I was very interested…in the creation of homes." Indeed, the arts and home making were inseparable in the minds of Jill Craigie and Lewis Mumford (1895-1990). Like William Morris, Mumford was an "encyclopaedist"—to use Michael Foot's term—"who seeks to embrace and relate all forms of knowledge; a popular philosopher, if you like, who does not care a fig for demarcation disputes with scientists, archaeologists, biologists and the rest." Biographer, literary critic, architectural historian, an anthropologist of sorts, an urbanist, Mumford was a synthesizer who helped Craigie fuse her feminism to her socialism to her desire to make a home. She met Mumford on one of his trips to England, and he inscribed several of his books to her, acknowledging in one of them *The Way We Live* (she put in her album about the making of the film a photograph of them together in Plymouth) and the affinity he felt for its director.

In *The Culture of the Cities* (1938), Jill underlined Mumford's description of premodern Europe that provided a "daily education of the senses." Echoing William Morris, Mumford evoked a vision of the "craftsman who had walked through fields and woods on holiday [and] came back to his stonecarving or his wood-working with a rich harvest of impressions." Mumford wrote prose deeply appealing to socialist sensibilities: "common men thought and felt in images more than in the verbal abstractions used by scholars: esthetic discipline might lack a name, but its fruits were everywhere visible. Did not the citizens of Florence vote as to type of column that was to be used on the Cathedral?" Courses in art, Mumford argued, were only necessary where the environment itself lacks an aesthetic. The filmmaker and homemaker in Craigie underlined declarations such as "verbal mastery cannot make up for sensory malnutrition."

Almost in the same breath as she spoke of Lewis Mumford, Craigie mentioned reading Sylvia Pankhurst's *The Suffragette Movement*, and "then I saw architecture from the feminine point of view." Craigie sensed the feminine in Mumford. In *The City in History* (1961), for example, he adopts a feminine view of architecture that Jill embodies in *The Way We Live*. In her film, Craigie uses women as a kind of community chorus to enact and comment on the consequences of male-inspired designs even as the film itself expresses a feminist temperament. Mumford, in other words, strengthened—he did not initiate—Craigie's thinking. She underlined the following passage because it validates her film:

> Woman's presence made itself felt in every part of the village: not least in its physical structures, with their protective enclosures, whose fuller symbolic meanings psychoanalysis has now tardily brought to light. Security, receptivity, enclosure, nurture—these functions belong to woman; they take structural expression in every part of the village, in the house the oven, byre and the bin, the cistern, the storage pit, the granary...the moats and inner spaces, from the atrium to the cloister. House, village, eventually the city itself, are woman writ large.

In a characteristic Mumford mannerism, he anticipates the reader's gasp at this sweeping generalization by nonchalantly referring to the "original bowl described in Greek myth, which was modelled on Aphrodite's breast."

Mumford's erudition, his conflation of history and psychology, and his search for relevance—he is always showing how we got to where we are now—had an overwhelming impact on a woman seeking to overcome, so to speak, the very momentum of history by making woman-centered films: "in the end Masculine processes over-rode by sheer dynamism the more passive life-nurturing activities that bore woman's imprint." Craigie underscored Mumford because he makes you see what he means: "one of the early Egyptian texts pictures Atun creating the universe out of his own body, by masturbation. The proud male could scarcely have used plainer words to indicate that, in the new scheme of life, woman no longer counted."

Among documentary filmmakers—mostly men—Craigie did not count. Of Paul Rotha, one of the few male documentary filmmakers she befriended, she said: "Both Paul and I were in bad for our socialism." But there is an edge even in her fondness for Rotha: "jolly pompous he was," she remembered. Humphrey's Jennings alluded to the clubbish atmosphere around "Rotha and other of Grierson's little boys who are still talking as loudly as possible about 'pure documentary' and 'realism' and other such systems of self-advertisement." Rotha was the reigning authority on documentary film at the time who wrote in *Documentary Film* (1939), prefaced by Grierson, that the genre is the "creative dramatisation of actuality and the expression of social analysis." Certainly *Out of Chaos* fulfills his desire for the voice-over narrator to be more informal, becoming a "part of the film rather than the detached 'Voice of God.'" Yet neither Rotha nor any other critic commented on the friendly female voice Craigie used for her art film, a voice sorely needed to balance Eric Newton's lugubrious delivery, but a voice evidently commanding little authority in a male-dominated society. Craigie also followed Rotha's suggestion to let the workers—or in the case of Henry Moore, the artist—speak for themselves in "simpler, more humble, and more honest speech" than the "professional commentator." She saw Rotha's *World of Plenty* (shot in 1942 but not released until 1943) and found its treatment of the problem of feeding the world "absolutely brilliant." As Rotha said of his own work in *Documentary Film*, "it caught all that was best in the determination of its time to make something better of the postwar world." Like his *Land of Promise* (1945), which employed a "full multi-voiced commentary, personalised in different characters" and a star actor, John Mills, *The Way We Live* blends together a central figure, a writer played by a professional actor, and his encounter with the broad range of people and professions representing themselves in postwar Plymouth. Like him, she was making "argument films." Yet Rotha does not acknowledge their affinity in *Documentary Film* or that *The Way We Live*, like *Land of Promise* which Jill saw in Rotha's company in a Leicester Square theatre), is "an argument on homes and houses." Asked nearly forty years later about the fraternity of documentary filmmakers, Craigie replied: "a woman didn't get any help from any of these people, you know, except the ones who made passes."

The resilience, persistence, and ingenuity Craigie exhibited were extraordinary. She realized that the best way to deal with her interest in women, in architecture, in art, and home making would be to capitalize on the keen public determination to rebuild the country. The British Council had sponsored two films in 1942, *New Towns for Old* and *When We Build Again* to explore the "opportunities that now exist for replanting towns after the war," and efforts to clear slums, rehouse people, and build new towns. Both architects and people who needed new housing were interviewed. But Jill had—of necessity—to do something more flashy and ambitious, for Del had told her that Rank would not be willing to fund any more short documentaries: "It is a great pity," he wrote her on 6 October 1944, "but such is the business! Moreover, I am dependent upon the leader of the Industry with whom lies the decision of investing money in productions."

Craigie began visiting the blitzed cities: Hull, Coventry, Durham, Liverpool, and Leeds. She chose Plymouth because of its "wonderful setting." Indeed, those in charge of reconstructing the city noted its picturesque qualities, especially the "seaboard of Devon and Cornwall and the heights of Dartmoor…the city is visibly and physically linked to our Coast and to one of our National Parks. To no other city in England do these two precious possessions approach so close." A film could take advantage of superb natural visuals in a "water-girt city standing on a tongue of land" like a Mediterranean town, with a "high bluff flanked by two harbours" and "dazzling cliffs." The city also had a Hoe, a piece of high ground that formed a platform or promenade by the sea, which Craigie would turn into a spectacular open-air stage. Plymouth, a great port city, had a historic backdrop perfectly suited for a film about a nation recovering and anticipating victory in war, since it was the home of Sir Francis Drake 1540-1596), a world famous explorer (the first Englishman to see the Pacific Ocean), the first Englishman to circumnavigate the world, and one of leading actors in the defeat of the Spanish Armada.

Plymouth also had a plan inspired, in part, by two of Craigie's architectural heroes, one of whom is quoted by the plan's authors:

> Perhaps in no direction has planning advanced more rapidly in recent years, than in the conception of the City as a human Community. Mr. Lewis Mumford has said that city planning and house planning have been and still are too mechanical: "we forget the human spirit and the changes of the human spirit to which everything should be adjusted, and we tinker too much with mere structures…. The City must be

planned for a community life...and not as a mere repository of industry."

One of the plan's authors, Patrick Abercrombie, had been the student of Sir Charles Reilly (1874-1948), whom Jill called "a great man" and the "father of town planning," whom she met, Michael Foot believes, at a London theatre or film fete. Reilly had almost single-handedly created the Liverpool School of Architecture in the early decades of the century—at a time when most architects shied away from academia as a career. He shifted the architect's focus away from the individual buildings to considering the larger questions of culture and how buildings could complement each other, and by his own example he urged his colleagues to forge more direct connections with the public by writing for popular publications such as *Country Life* and the *Manchester Guardian*. He wrote and planned for ordinary people, not just his peers or his clients. Most important, for Craigie, Reilly insisted that architecture could only thrive in an atmosphere of healthy criticism. No style, no architect, including himself, was sacrosanct. Reilly, in short, suited Craigie right down to the ground. At a reception sponsored by his school of architecture, the students even designed the menu cards.

Reilly's celebration of community suffuses the Plymouth plan, although it did not—Craigie recognized—go nearly as far as her hero in implementing the "village green" concept, in which houses were arranged around greens "as in pre-Industrial Revolution England, and the greens themselves arranged like the petals of a flower round a community building, the modern equivalent of the village inn." As Craigie described it:

> we should build round a green, mixed developments where the people looked at each other instead of everyone keeping themselves to themselves...you should leave great gaps for organized developments because you can't cater for the diversity of human need all in one go...if people all face each other, the children can play in safety on the green...their backs are facing the roads, and that is where your tradesmen come. He says if you keep yourself to yourself, you don't all talk to each other, you don't create neighbours, your children don't mix.

The village green, moreover, promoted "mixed development," a natural socialist society, Craigie thought, because they're all dependent upon one another

> Like in the Cotswold town, where you see the lawyer living next to the ironmonger, or the blacksmith as he was in those days...the squire and the vicar might live separately, but the rest of the classes were all jum-

bled up together…The workman's cottage was certainly next door to the very grand Queen Anne establishments belonging to the doctor or the lawyer.

The rhetoric of the Plymouth plan was pure Reilly and would provide the context for Craigie's film. The plan spoke the Reilly/Morris language, deploring the consequences of an Industrial Revolution that had destroyed the coherence of society and created a "labour pool for the large industrial works—soulless and meaningless." The plan evoked the solidarity stimulated by the Blitz: "Experience in the war has exemplified the fact that when the cause of the community is at stake, individualism must be subordinated." Rebuilding Plymouth, in other words, would be as heroic and as concerted an effort as fighting the war had been. The prewar city's haphazard, sprawling, "discordant development" would give way to a harmony based on the "human, personal scale." A muted Morris note is struck in the plan's overture that it "should be possible to incorporate art in the design and decoration of the home."

Reilly had retired from teaching in 1934 because of a heart condition, but he was still very much on the scene and keenly interested not just in Craigie's film but also in Craigie. Exactly when they met is not clear. MacQuitty, who would again act as Craigie's on site producer, remembered they went to see Reilly who was "full of enthusiasm and helpful ideas." In Craigie's copy of his book, *Representative British Architects of the Present Day* (1931), the author wrote this inscription:

> The owner of this book is Jill Craigie, in my opinion not only a lovely creature but far cleverer than any of the architects described here. I have fallen for her in spite of being in my 70's—deeply!
>
> Charles Reilly
> Jan 1945

By the time Jill met Charles Reilly she had read her man—prompting another inscription in her copy of his autobiography, *Scaffolding in the Sky* (1938):

> I have just heard, dear Jill, bought this book before she knew me & apparently has kept it since. It makes me very happy to hear this.
>
> Charles Reilly
> Jan 1946

In his autobiography, Reilly claims to have been "a very square toed person" in his youth. If that is so, he certainly matured into a well rounded William Morris man (the Labour Party at its December 1944 conference passed a resolution approving his "ideas for community planning)." He relished his socialist principles, attacking the "individualism of scrambling competitive commerce" that ruined the coherence of English towns and despoiled the countryside, and he savored a sense of humor and of sexual adventure. A man of "baroque instincts—so it was said at the conferral of his Liverpool University honorary degree—and a seductive performer, he had a charm and guile that might almost be called feminine (if such an expression can be used now without giving offense). Confronted with a young woman who refused to relinquish her lease in a building wanted by the architecture school, Reilly felt he should get to know her better:

> Then I discovered one day she was a suffragette. I promptly became the equivalent of one too. Of course I had sympathies in that direction. Who would not with such spirit and such eyes? Indeed, I began to like my enemy very much. I set about to like her more, a little deliberately I fear with my end in view. I was successful but I found I liked her more and more. One day we went out together to telephone the Vice-Chancellor that at last the way was clear. We went to a little shop with the telephone on the counter. There was only one chair. While I was talking to that grave and rather choleric administrative head of the University and telling him the obstacle had now been removed, the obstacle herself was sitting on my knee and tickling my free ear.

Then there was Doonie, the wife of Albert Lipczinski, an artist working in Liverpool. Husband and wife visited Reilly and wife for two weeks, with Albert afterwards going out with friends while Doonie returned to Reilly, whose wife was away at the time. "The result can be imagined," Reilly confessed:

> Doonie and I became very fond indeed of each other, to say the least of it, and we have remained so to this day. When I got in from the University on the first day my wife was back, I found her with Doonie in tears in her arms on the floor of the sitting-room. There had clearly been some sort of explanation and Dorothy had taken Doonie to her heart where she has remained ever since. Indeed, she is now as much my wife's friend as mind. It has been the same with others. My women friends have become hers in every case. If it has been a strain on her

sometimes she has not shown it. Clearly I owe her a very deep debt for this. Few women could or would have acted so wisely.

Reilly is not reticent about describing his "women friends" in other equally remarkable episodes. So he has to be added to a long list of admirers that Jill juggled while still married to Jeffrey Dell. That romance was on the architect's mind is evident in his inscription in Craigie's copy of *The Reilly Plan*:

> I wish Jill Craigie was part of my plan. She would be in any real "new way of life."
>
> Charles Reilly
> Jan 1946

The pilgrimage to Plymouth promised much. Patrick Abercrombie proved easy to work with: "It was a great triumph to get him to appear in the film," Craigie remembered, "though he was glad enough to be in it because he liked being made up. It's extraordinary how all men seem to like being made up." J. Paton Watson, the city engineer, and co-author of the Plymouth plan, was "extremely efficient…the whole town was very ordered. Everyone did what he said. He was a bit of a dictator." There was the natural link to America in the story of the Plymouth pilgrims, and the "Astors were big names," Craigie said, "I thought this would appeal to the Rank organisation." It did. The outspoken and controversial Nancy Astor (1879-1964), an American from Virginia and the first woman to take a seat in Parliament, was always in the news. Her confrontations with Churchill were legendary. If she had him for a husband, she baited the prime minister, she would poison him. If he was her husband, he'd take the poison, Churchill retorted. She had run into trouble in the 1930s for allegedly pro-Nazi sympathies. An aristocratic Southerner, a Tory, and a militant Protestant, she attacked Catholics relentlessly in Parliament. But she was a gallant and witty campaigner, devoted to the people of Plymouth, and during the war exhibited a Churchillian courage as she walked among the ruins, rallied the citizens of a city that had been bombed as badly as London, and made her home available to wounded serviceman—including American blacks—whom she urged in her usual robust fashion not to dwell on their injuries but to get on with the war. If by 1944, she had alienated so many members of her own Conservative Party that her husband persuaded her to retire, she nevertheless retained the considerable affection of her constituency and the lively interest of the country.

Nancy's husband, Waldorf Astor, then Lord Mayor of Plymouth, endorsed the plan, declaring that Plymouth would be "rebuilt as a unity." Important local political figures such as Leslie Hore-Belisha (1893-1957) opposed the plan, and he decided not to appear in the film, Craigie said, when she told him he might look like the villain. The "mood of the moment" was socialistic. As an interviewer said to Craigie, Lord Astor in her film talks like Karl Marx. Craigie added: "later, Lord Astor advocates nationalisation of land, and my goodness they did it at Plymouth. They owned the land; they owned the whole centre of the city. So it was Tories and Labour thinking alike at that moment."

With Del Giudice's help, the Rank organization got behind the film. But only just—explains Geoffrey Macnab. Although discussion of a "better Britain" certainly engaged the public and books on the subject became best sellers, there was little evidence that "enthusiasm for town planning extended to the cinema." And as with *Out of Chaos*, Craigie's plan to use "real people" and actors, to script the film but also to base the dialogue on what people actually said and did, was risky. "Nor did this early British attempt at neo-realism, at combining fact and fiction, real life with invented drama, seem to have much box-office allure," Macnab concludes. For the moment, however, Rank evidently held in check his "patriarchal conservatism."

Not so Nancy Astor. As Craigie's film began to take shape in May and June of 1945, Lady Astor became alarmed as she saw Jill honing in on in the collectivist aspects of the Plymouth plan. As John Grigg notes in *Nancy Astor: A Lady Unashamed*, she was a "social reformer who felt that society should be improved largely on private initiative, with the State helping but not taking over." More partisan than her husband, she accused Craigie of making, in effect, a Labour Party film. Perhaps Lady Astor had heard that the crewmembers on Craigie's film were spending their time campaigning for a Labour Party victory in the 1945 elections. At any rate, Lady Astor called John Davis and asked him to get Arthur Rank to stop the film. William MacQuitty remembered being summoned back to London for a meeting with Rank and John Davis. Liam showed them the wonderful press the film was getting. "Look at these John," Rank said. "We're too late." Del congratulated MacQuitty on his quick work, but he decided to see Lady Astor, figuring she had only begun to fight. He showed up at her house without an invitation and was received rudely. But the persistent MacQuitty said he had come to show Lady Astor the script containing the "key scene" in which her husband appeared. He followed her to lunch, noticing that both Abercrombie and Paton-Waton were there. Evidently the film was under discussion. Lady Astor abruptly asked MacQuitty "What is it? He showed her the script. She glanced at it and said, "What is that bitch up to?" She thought of Craigie as a Russian (Craigie's mother was Russian), MacQuitty later said, and a revolutionary one at that, no doubt. MacQuitty reiterated that Jill had made sure Lord Astor had "full recognition for his part in the Plymouth plan." Lady Astor told him to "sit down and have some lunch." He hadn't come for lunch, MacQuitty said, "but I will take a drumstick." She laughed. MacQuitty wisely withdrew.

Michael Foot remembered Jill's stories about Lady Astor's intervention and that Jill nevertheless retained considerable respect and affection for the first woman to hold a Parliamentary seat. "The first thing she said to me was 'For God's sake, take my husband from me," Jill recalled. "She faced, alone at first, both the ridicule and the freezing hatred of the male House of Commons, Michael Foot wrote. "She bombarded the ramparts of prejudice with just the right combination of insolence, scorn, repartee and courage." Lady Astor never hesitated to attack Churchill, who had been one of the archenemies of Votes for Women. Craigie would also have learned from Foot and others what a great advocate for Plymouth Lady Astor had always been. "Almost my first memory of campaigning was the 1919 election when my father ran against Lady Astor," Foot said. Their rivalry had been friendly and she shared Isaac Foot's "favourite Puritan causes—temperance, anti-Popery, Plymouth's greatness as a Protestant City." In Michael Foot's words, she was a "Daniel come to judgement: better still, it was Portia herself with a touch of the Queen of Sheba."

Craigie's accounts to film historians such as Drazin, Macnab, and Philip Kemp detail only a confrontation involving herself, Rank, and Davis. Davis said the film was not going to make any money. Of course not, Craigie countered. It was a "prestige" item. Davis scoffed. Then Craigie showed the press cuttings to Rank that praised him for making a film about their problems; she explained how she had "turned Plymouth upside down"—even getting the police to stop traffic for the production; she pointed to the admiring notices of her as a woman director given her opportunity by Rank. "You're going to look awfully foolish if you stop it now," she told them. Jill then saw Rank turn to Davis and say, "You see John; it can't be stopped." She looked at Rank and could see he was "delighted." Patrick Abercrombie wrote Craigie to congratulate her "on the conquest of Lady A."

MacQuitty mentions Del Giudice as playing the pivotal role in Craigie's career in this period. Davis seemed determined to destroy Del, whose extravagance Davis could not tolerate. As MacQuitty said, Del never invited you to dinner; it was always to a "ban-quet." At any rate, Del certainly had to do all in his power to justify his support of Craigie's film. He would have presented her film to Del, Rank, and Davis as a kind of community crusade unfamiliar to the film industry. As Craigie said:

> I wanted to show how.... planning and housing related to the people and especially to women, and I wanted to show the architects what people thought and I wanted to show the people what the architects thought and try to get a synthesis out of that...it was considered an absolutely mad idea at the time and indeed...a commercial element in the industry was strongly opposed to it.

Especially mad was Jill's proposal to present the film as a "second feature"—that is part of a double bill in theaters and not as a documentary short. As a good socialist, she wanted plenty of ordinary people in it, but as a professional filmmaker she made sure they got "tested," and the less self-conscious "naturals" were chosen. They got into the "spirit of it," she recalled when they invented some of their own dialogue. Mrs. Copperwheat, for example, was a war widow who enjoyed doing the film. "It did her a lot of good," Craigie said. "It was very therapeutic for her." Craigie saw no reason why so-called ordinary people could not be entertaining for a feature film audience—indeed she found them far more flexible and spontaneous than the upper class and military officers. Some of the cast appeared by accident—for example, when Craigie spotted an American sailor, a good dancer, and discovered he was eager to be in the film.

The campaign quality of the film is best demonstrated in the closing scenes which the city's young people carry banners demonstrating in favor of the Plymouth plan. Here Craigie capitalized on public sentiment to organize and create a scene that became part of the public participation in the plan. *The Way We Live* becomes a moment in film, and in Craigie's life, when her politics and her filmmaking fuse into a kind of apotheosis.

With a rousing overture, the documentary opens with this bid for attention:

> This film is made for the people of the blitz in the hope that their newly built cities will be worthy of their fortitude.

The first shot is an aerial view that rapidly closes in on Plymouth as a voice over narrator announces, "this is a tale of a town and of the town's folk," followed by scenes identifying the Lord Mayor and the corporation, big business, little business, the fishermen, the mothers, and the Copperwheats." Each group turns to look at the audience as they are identified, almost like actors bowing as the narrator continues: "But the heroes or villains—according to your point of view—are two men with a plan: J. Paton-Watson, the city engineer, and Professor Abercrombie" (looking very professorial indeed with his monocle). "What they have to offer is something of a challenge to the way we live." Up comes the music as the credits roll over the model buildings of the Plymouth plan.

The tale then switches to the voice over of a soldier/writer returning home on a troop ship docking in Southhampton to the sounds of a welcoming band. "What now?" the writer wonders. No home, no job, he limps disconsolately along streets with drab shops. Patriotic messages about reconstruction do not move him. "We never talked that way in the desert," he notes, although the "boys talked a lot about their towns, their home towns." As he muses on his need to begin writing, the tune the band played—"Pack up your troubles in an old kit bag"—keeps coming back to him to his annoyance. He looks in a shop window at books about town planning, including *The Reilly Plan* and Paton-Watson's and Abercrombie's Plymouth plan. He writes to the city engineer but does not expect an answer. He visits a newspaper office and is told his story will be dull and he better put some sex in it. Abercrombie will be too busy to see him, another asserts. Yet another suggests the plan won't come to anything anyway. Criticism and cynicism build up the same idea as *Out Chaos*: a heroic effort is always required to overturn received opinion and inertia.

After hassles getting a train ticket, he arrives dreaming of summer in Devon and finds instead a gloomy, rainy setting. Watching from a taxi he spots an attractive woman walking on the street and has to remind himself of his business—"still it might be useful to get the feminine angle," he thinks. Now the full sight of Plymouth's destruction strikes him. It all seems even grimmer to him after talking to an American sailor, who barely registers the Englishman's observation that the pilgrims left from Plymouth. "So I've heard," the sailor says.

The next day, the writer walks out to a magnificent view of the Hoe and the harbor. A line of poetry occurs to him "masts with sunset fire" and he remarks, "that's one way of looking at it." But as the scene shifts to the streets, he observes the lack of gardens, no place for children to play, and reflects on the city's glorious history, the Elizabethans and Drake—but "half the time one looks to the past instead of facing up to the present," he points out. In some places the city is so congested that there are "230 to the acre." Human beings living together like flies in conditions as primitive and less healthy than the Middle Ages, he observes, as the film silently shows crowded streets, small family kitchens, where every space is taken by children trying to play games or sitting on floors (there is little furniture) and mothers in the midst of the chaos attempting to make meals. These claustrophobic, constricting conditions are juxtaposed against Plymouth's triumphs as a port city, the gateway to America and the world, its election of Lady Astor, a Virginian, its natural advantages in "rolling farmlands, shimmering streams, lush valleys, old world villages, winding lanes, and a windswept moor. It might be the most beautiful setting in the world." It has been marred (the music sounds discordant, the narrator disgusted) by unplanned housing, sprawling suburbs until...[the sounds of bombers are heard and the scene shifts to an aerial view as though seen from the bombers]. Explosions, fires, roar across the screen, with scenes of houses and other buildings ripped apart. The voice over switches to the sneering voice of Lord Haw Haw (William Joyce) whose wartime broadcasts taunted the British people. "Plymouth," he announces, is "beyond repair."

The scene shifts to a long line of weary people, including the Copperwheat family, who are without homes. Mr. Copperwheat, a dockyard worker, and his wife have three children and their Granny. They are trucked to Mrs. Hines's home where they have to make do in very cramped conditions—the oldest daughter will sleep in the kitchen, Granny and the two younger girls will sleep with their mother in the bedroom, and Mr. Copperwheat in the only other space, a makeshift sitting room. All have to move very quietly so as not to disturb their hostess, who lives directly below them. But it still seems "paradise" compared to the shelter, one of the girls says.

As the family settles down to make a home, shots of a devastated Plymouth dominate the screen, and inside of one ruin Paton-Watson is shown saying this "waste" can also be an opportunity. The improvised market, for example, has the advantage of bringing all the shops together and out of the rain. Services are held in the ruins of St. Andrews. The children now use the wrecked city as a playground, and rebuilding becomes an industry in itself. Miraculously much of old historic Plymouth, like the Barbicon, survives. And the homeless spend their summer dancing on the Hoe. "There was a new spirit in the air and a new movement afoot." A tight close-up shows Paton-Watson explaining his plan to destroy the "warrens" people live in and the traffic bottlenecks. The writer, interviewing Paton-Watson, wonders if his ambitions plans are not rather "remote." Paton-Watson tells the incredulous writer that he should visit a "mother's meeting" at a housing estate. There he hears their complaints about houses situated too far from shopping, inadequate washing facilities, poor plumbing (they have to fill baths with buckets of water), not enough rooms for larger families, and children have nowhere to play. The writer then presents the village green concept to the women—for the first time looking comfortable and establishing some rapport with the women. Walking away from the meeting, now striding with a sense of purpose he did not have after leaving the troop ship, the writer reflects: "What was it Shaw said? 'Man's house hasn't changed as much in a thousand years as a woman's bonnet in a score of weeks. yet when he goes out to kill he carries a marvel of mechanism."

Viewers today will easily miss the significance of the village green scene—unless they are look quite closely at Abercrombie's sketches of the new city. They have a monumental look to them that diminishes Reilly's idea of a community planned on the human scale. Craigie later admitted that she had "inserted" this scene "regardless as to what anyone in Plymouth thought. It was the one bit of cheating I did in a kind of way, because the rest of it did come from the people."

Craigie's feminism fortifies Shaw's sense of how women innovate and shape the domestic architecture of life by shooting the Copperwheats around a table, with Alice, the eldest daughter, standing at the rear of a table around which the family sits, the mother knitting at the head of the table responding to her children, and the father engrossed in his paper. He comes into the picture only when his wife questions him to make sure he has filled in the paperwork for a prefabricated house. Alice, who dominates the scene, asks permission to go out, which her father grants as long as she is back by ten. The music heard when the father briefly turns on the radio (shut off because it disturbs another daughter doing homework) segues to a scene with dancing on the Hoe.

The next sequence shifts back and forth between Alice and her girlfriend Dorothy and the sailors eyeing them. Alice turns one down, and stands there in smug British reserve. But before she can protest an American sailor takes her hand and swings her out into a dance. He is so good that Alice wishes she could go on dancing in the open air all night. "And dancing and dancing and dancing on the Hoe, just as they did all through the ages," the voice over of the writer is heard, quoting Shakespeare's lines about this "other Eden…this little world…this precious stone…this earth…this England." The grand words, however, are set against the unsightly ravages of war and its aftermath, which in turn give way to Lord Astor's quoting "to each according to his need. We want to build so that everyone will have a chance of leading a full life. That is the philosophy of our plan." "But it is really practical,"the writer wants to know. A town counselor leaves that for him to judge.

Representing the plan is Patrick Abercrombie—shown now on the heights of Plymouth looking over and walking through the city. "Nobody quite knew what the professor was up to," the writer reports. Shots of the plan's sketches, emphasizing the importance of squares and centers punctuate his walk, and the music rises as Abercrombie's thoughts about the coordination of horizontal and vertical masses (to give the city an interesting skyline) begin to soar—until they are brought to ground by the voice over narrator: "But what was planning a city compared to the difficulty of finding a house?" The Copperwheats are shown touring a model house (the father has filled out twenty-nine forms so far). The Copperwheats comment on every aspect of the house, thinking in terms of their daily lives—quite a different view from the planners, a point that the film is at pains to show. As the family goes on about the cramped space ("no place to swing a cat") Alice admires herself in the mirror. She is the most aesthetic member of the family—and clearly the one who most wants more out of her surroundings.

The experience of individuals and families gives way to a collective scene of people assembling for a presentation of the plan. As Abercrombie begins to explain why the city cannot be rebuilt as it once was, a woman turns to her male companion and says, "I hope he's not going to be a bore." Returning to the past would be a "fake," he says, rejecting the idea of taking a "snip here, a snip there." Much too cautious. "What is a town planner?" one fellow asks another. "A fellow who plans towns." "Extraordinary." The third approach, Abercrombie continues, is to make the "best possible use of the land for the community as a whole." Mr. Copperwheat comments to his wife: "I hope I haven't missed my pint for nothing," Craigie realized that as a "second feature" her audience might well be saying the same thing about her film. If "movies must move," she had to break up Abercrombie's lecture not only with these brief interjectory scenes but also with commentary that undercut the film's lecture-like format.

Abercrombie then projects onto a screen maps that move with lines and circles that demonstrate the haphazard development he compares to "measles." He arouses an audience member's wrath when he suggests that in order to tie developments together into a community part of Cornwall will have to become Devonshire. Abercrombie and Patton-Watson handle the rapid-fire queries and criticism by showing how unplanned sites will only make the entire area worse off, especially in the destruction of the countryside in which villages have been torn in half and the agricultural economy harmed. Similarly, planning is needed to cope with the cars which now clog access to the city and have caused accidents that took more lives than the bombing did. Drawings, photographs, newsreel footage, diagrams—indeed every kind of visual lightens the load of Abercrombie's lecture and illustrates his argument that other countries have implemented such plans. "Why should we remain behind the times?" he asks. The audience assents, although one man is heard snoring. "All we have tried to do is plan the ideal city the way we would plan an ideal home." This vision of a city with "spaciousness and beauty for all" is greeted with cheers. as the meeting breaks up, Mr. Copperwheat says, "it sounds all right, but who's going to pay for it?"

The pro and the antis are pictured in scenes shifting back and forth debating the plan—women seated around a sewing circle, fishermen working on nets, small and big business representatives, and Lord Astor speaking to the Lords endorsing the plan. "Such was the power of the Lords," the writer comments, that "nothing happened." He then encounters Alice, determined to find out "what she thought." In front of the plan's model Alice says she does not think it matters, and her sailor companion says "they don't have the kind of go ahead that Americans do." The writer tries to make them understand that "they" is "we." They can have the plan if they want it. But the young couple simply does not seem to care. "So much easier to kill an idea than look into it," the aggrieved writer charges.

Then the film presents the council's discussion and adoption of the plan. Everything they said in that meeting, they had said at a previous council meeting—I didn't cheat at all," Craigie said "and I wanted to be absolutely fair to everyone, and let them all have their heads, and I did—and just left it at that." It is a rousing, contentious discussion that eventually results in endorsement of the plan. Still nothing happened, the writer reports. The community's mounting frustration is exemplified in Mr. Copperwheat's fretful speech about the crowded living conditions, but Alice interrupts to say she is going on the Hoe. Her father doubts her word, she invites him to come along, and to her dismay, he does, accompanied by his wife. A silent choreography then ensues as Alice walks with her parents on the Hoe and surreptitiously signals the sailors to keep their distance. The Copperwheats sit down, joined by Dorothy, and engage in desultory conversation with Alice wistfully suggesting it might be rather nice to live in America. "Well, suppose you bring him over and let us meet him," Mrs. Copperwheat says to her daughter, who feigns surprise, with Dorothy helping her out by saying the sailors are her friends. But Mrs. Copperwheat is not fooled and sends the girls off to bring the boys to meet her and Mr. Copperwheat, who asks his wife how she knew "something was going on." "I think I know my own daughter," she replies. The wary father says, "with her looks you can't be too careful." "Perhaps you can, George," his wife replies.

It is difficult to believe any male filmmaker would have put such a scene into a film about the rebuilding of Plymouth, linking this young, beautiful girl's restlessness and desire to see the world and to make contact with it to the spirit of adventure that created Plymouth in the first place. Her father is proud to think that his family might have fought alongside Drake, but he is quite complacent about his place in Plymouth and cannot begin to imagine newer worlds. Alice's younger sister has already expressed a wish to go out on her own, no matter where, just to escape the confinement of postwar Plymouth. It is not difficult to see how Craigie projected her own biography and beliefs into the yearnings of these young women. Even though they have no conscious interest in the Plymouth plan, they represent the new spirit it has tried to express. Watching his daughter Mr. Copperwheat is suddenly aroused, realizing how little he has come to expect out of life from the "dole, then there's the war, then there'll be exports...one day I suppose the workers will wake up."

Mr. Copperwheat's outburst provides the transition to the writer's voice-over explanation that "out of the growing discontent new leaders arose to fire the citizens with hope," followed immediately by a shot of an announcement: "The Labour Candidate Michael Foot Speaking To-Night." The next shot pans over an attentive and receptive audience, including the applauding Copperwheats, before Foot is shown, standing dressed in a neat double breasted pinstripe suit, speaking in full flow about the rebuilding of Plymouth: "We say the burden must be shared," he argues, so that the people of Plymouth are not left to pay for the reconstruction while other cities in Britain that escaped bombing remit nothing. He is stiff, his hands hanging somewhat awkwardly at his side, but then the angle changes to a tight close-up, in which the focus is on his determination and forceful words: "By this plan we can make ours one of the most beautiful cities in the whole wide world." Craigie thought, "thank God, there's a Labour chap who is actually interested in aesthetics."

Although the films shows a ballot marked Foot which signifies his election, attention shifts to exploring the period of anti-climax, when people seemed "apathetic" and weary of still living in their bombed-out city. The dejected writer strolls on the Hoe, gazes at a war memorial, and notices "something odd." Coming into camera is a banner—and then several others—held aloft by young people. Each banner has a message: "LESS MONOTONY PLEASE," "PREMISES NOT PROMISES," "BIGGER HOUSES," "ROADS DESIGNED FOR SAFETY," "YOUTH WANTS A THEATRE." Groups with banners parade through the town with a marching band shot at eye level to create a sense of the action being carried to the audience; a high angle shot shows them crossing a pedestrian bridge with banners aloft to the sky; a low-angle shot displays the bright banners emerging out of shadows—a stark contrast to dark interior city walls. Soldiers, sailors, scouts, and other boys and girls clubs converge in a collective demonstration that fills the main street lined with crowds on both sides. The film ends with this—panoply (MacQuitty puts their number at three thousand), with the London Symphony Orchestra's triumphant finale, and the writer's concluding words: "The cities of tomorrow. Who can tell what they will be. Their story is still being written by the citizens of today."

Jill's Craigie's democratic/socialist aesthetic is especially striking when compared with another woman documentary film-maker, a genius at handling crowds, at displaying the dynamism of youth and flag flying patriotism, and superb at having the visuals tell the story—at making movies move. But in Leni Riefenstahl's films, the crowds gather around the supreme leader, and the aesthetic is fascist; the sense of community is centered on adoration of an individual In *Triumph of the Will*, physical and mental strength are equated with power, and there is no place for conflicting arguments. Indeed, Hitler's triumph is presented as the triumph of unity over criticism. Jill Craigie's aesthetic, on the other hand, is all about debate and disagreement. Michael Foot may be the hero of the moment, but he is heard speaking only for a minute. Heroes only get cameo treatment.

The final moments of the film grew out of Craigie's discussion with a cynical group of young people who told her that the plan would never happen. Like all good agitators, Craigie provoked them:

> "What are YOU going to do about it?" I said democracy is rather like marriage. It only works if both sides work. And out of this discussion they said: "well we'd better have an exhibition—better have a protest march." And it was their idea…. The council stopped all the traffic for us.

"You had the city in your pocket in May/June 1945, didn't you?" an interviewer asked. "Yes, Craigie agreed. With the making of the film, with the Labour triumph in the election, with the arrival of Michael Foot, she felt the millennium had come.

"No Socialist who saw it will forget the blissful dawn of July 1945," wrote Michael Foot: "The great war in Europe had ended; the lesser war in Asia might be ending soon. This background to the scene in Britain naturally deepened the sense of release and breath-taking opportunity. And those who had served the British Labour movement for generations, renewing their faith after each disaster, in 1919, 1926 and 1931, had their own special cause for exultation." Craigie had come to the party late, so to speak, through Malcolm Macdonald and then Michael Foot, but she felt the full force of that recovery from catastrophe. In 1919, Malcolm's father had led the party to a crushing defeat. In 1924, as Prime Minister in a minority government, Ramsey Macdonald pursued an extremely cautious program that deeply disappointed members of his own party and ended two years later with a decisive Conservative victory. Worst of all, Macdonald and his Cabinet had failed to capitalize on their 1929 majority, and by 1931 had drastically cut public expenditures and united with Conservatives to form a national party. His brilliant early years as the first leader to make Labour the largest party in Parliament were eclipsed by policies and alliances deemed as anti-Labour by his former colleagues and supporters. During the Second World War, Aneurin Bevan feared that the Labour ministers in Churchill's coalition government might make the Macdonald mistake yet again, which is why he aggressively advanced the view that the country would abandon Churchill's old-fashioned heroics as soon as the war was over. Bevan stood virtually alone—"against all odds and orthodox prophecies" that presumed the popular Churchill would model himself after the Lloyd George of 1918 who united peoples and parties into one patriotic government. But Bevan had been right: the attack on Britain had focused the people on the "promise of a new society. Suddenly the vision of the Socialist pioneers had been given substance and historic impetus by the radical political ferment of wartime." Indeed, the "discipline of war could be used to buttress the necessary planning for the future." Labour would not err again by eviscerating reformist expectations. "When the scale of the Labour Party's victory became known on the night of 26 July, Foot reports, "bonfires were lit, people danced in the streets, and young and old crowded into halls all over the country to acclaim their elected standard bearers." Craigie's dancing scenes on the Hoe, seen in the light of the 1945 victory, seemed prophetic.

The Way We Live premiered at the Plymouth Odeon (a Rank theatre) on 29 July 1946 to an enthusiastic audience (the city continues to show the film at periodic intervals as a pivotal part of its history). A proud William MacQuitty pointed out in his memoir that in September the film "received outstanding praise" as the first documentary shown at the Cannes Film Festival. The film accomplished a "very difficult thing," one reviewer noted, weaving "out of a large number of threads a pattern of democratic discussion ranging over the whole area of Plymouth and its surroundings." The *Times* critic concluded: "the film on the whole is admirable in being at once generously ardent in spirit and nearly impartial in argument."

Yet John Davis had tried to kill the film by showing it in an East End theatre where he knew the audience would not have the patience to sit through a documentary. "I was depressed because it got booed, got the boot," Craigie said. But then she was told, "that's nothing. They threw tomatoes at the screen at *Henry V!* According to Geoffrey Macnab, *Observer* critic C.A. Lejeune "rallied her colleagues to the cause," hailing the film as "intelligent, thoughtful, comprehensive," and *The Way We Live* did find a distributor.

However, Charles Drazin suggests how Davis's opposition to both of Craigie's documentaries damaged her career:

> *Out of Chaos* would have announced the arrival of a gifted and sensitive filmmaker had any company been willing to distribute it.... The distributors were reluctant to show films they did not consider to be "popular entertainment". Their lack of support is a major reason why Craigie, who was a fine filmmaker, is so little known as such today.

Unfortunately, most documentary film historians—many of whom have probably not had access to her work—do not acknowledge her. Paul Rotha in *Documentary Film* provides her with this mixed tribute:

> To Jill Craigie went the credit for getting the film industry, in the form of the Rank Organisation through Two Cities, to back *The Way We Live*.... A far more expensive and larger production than a M.O.I. [Ministry of Information] film, it enjoyed a considerable success despite initial opposition from the associated Rank cinemas. For continuity the film resorted to the well-worn device of the visitor, a journalist.... the family who were the principal protagonists were adequately directed, but the film as a whole broke no new ground.

Craigie herself disclaimed originality and often called her films the work of an amateur, but then she always measured herself against the highest standard. Even so, she saw what made her different from Rotha:

> I wanted to translate my films into more human terms. I tried to that, to have characters, real people in it. His [Rotha's] was an intellectual argument, wasn't it, *Land of Promise*. You can't say mine's an intellectual argument, although it's a bit of a mess.

The "bit of a mess" had to do with her ambition to cram so much into one film—not just to show but also to activate the "interaction between building and planning and families."

Ambition and self-doubt tore at Jill Craigie's sensibility: "I was nervous. I looked self-confident in front of these chaps, but I wasn't.... Once I'd finished the film, of course, I could only see the mistakes and I was horrified. I wasn't good enough, in fact. I could have been good enough." She regretted that the studios provided no opportunities for women to learn the technicalities of film-making, to move up the ranks from tea boy to cameramen to directors of B pictures, mastering their trade. The war had abruptly opened a window of opportunity that just as quickly closed when the war ended. Such sudden breaks for women had no "roots." When she offered to become part of the production team for Rank's *March of Time* newsreel/documentary series—"in any capacity...I was absolutely black-balled out of the industry, I couldn't get work anywhere," she told Charles Drazin. Craigie believed that her outspoken socialism harmed her in an industry dominated by Conservatives—an obstacle she would continue to confront throughout the 1950s. Although she bluntly called her films "bad and amateur," she mitigated that harsh judgment by observing "they weren't nearly so bad and amateur as some of the boys' first films."

In *The Women's Companion to International Film,* cinema historians Annette Kuhn and Susannah Radstone single out Jill Craigie's "ability to bring out the best in 'ordinary people'" and her "political commitment," without clearly noting how remarkably she was able to blend her feminism and socialism in *The Way We Live.* In *Women Filmmakers and Their Films,* critic Philip Kemp ably captures what makes her distinctive:

> *The Way We Live* was something quite new: it set out to show how planning, that panacea of the postwar Labour government, affected the lives of 'ordinary people'—and how they, in their turn, could influence the planning process.... But more, it was an exceptional—and in Britain, virtually unheard of—example of filmmaking as activism, the creative and political processes intertwining and advancing each other in a way that even the Soviet filmmakers of the 1920s had only rarely achieved.

Children of the Ruins

In *To Be A Woman: The Life of Jill Craigie*, I tell the demoralizing story of her failure after the war to secure employment at major film studios as a director/writer. She wrote several fine scripts for feature films but managed to produce only three more documentaries, *Children of the Ruins* (1948), *To Be A Woman* (1951), and *Who Are the Vandals?* (1967), although in her eighties she would return with surprising vigor to the documentary form in *Two Hours From London* (1994), her impassioned account of the Serbian/Croatian war.

In 1947, UNESCO, commissioned Craigie to direct a short documentary, *Children of the Ruins*, about the impact of the war on youth across Europe. Her ten-minute short, a production of the Crown Film Unit, presents provocative images of children playing in rubble, crouching in rags, emaciated and forlorn, stretching out their hands for food. A voice, clearly Craigie's, asks whether the war effort tended to rate industrial might more highly than concern for human values. Shots shift to children in crowded, dingy, poorly lit schoolrooms—"as if they could really learn this way," remarks a male voice. The situation in the U.S. is better, the narrator continues, but scenes of picketing teachers and headlines about strikes emphasize their low salaries and the teacher shortage. Children are shown going to school barefoot. The plight of girls in other parts of the world (India, for example) is such that they receive "hardly any education at all. "A whole generation was brought up," says the male voice—"or shall we say dragged up," Craigie's voice interrupts—with the "consequences of war." Children are dehumanized and transformed by the war machinery, the narrator notes, as brief shots of Hitler and his slavishly saluting youth corps dominate the screen. Amid scenes of book burning, the narrator quotes Isaac Newton's view that to destroy books is to destroy reason itself. Since the war advances have been made, but three-quarters of the world's children are brought up uneducated. Not the destruction of the cities but the break-up of homes and families is the greatest tragedy of war, the narrator insists.

"The whole world was on the move." Craigie's film portrays the history of the 20th century as the saga of displaced peoples. Shots of children digging up the bricks between streetcar tracks, hauling water in decimated landscapes, and bearing huge bundles on their backs, are juxtaposed with the narrator's observation: "To be young and to live meant to be old beyond one's years." Children learn survival skills, but "what is going on in their minds?" The film's shots of children clamoring for bowls and cups and of camps with no parents suggest that the work of relief organizations seems noble but horrendously inadequate,

This world problem becomes the focus of a UNESCO conference—"What, another committee?—Craigie's voice breaks in. "And what's it all going to cost?" The male voice replies: "Well, what would you do?" The propagandistic intent of the film now emerges: UNESCO thinks of the world as "one place" and aims to provide the "tools of learning" (pencils and books) and teachers. "If we have a scrap of humanity," the narrator emphasizes, the crisis of the world's children cannot be ignored. "Difficult to feel for people when they are so far away, but our neighbors matter." Shots of a devastated Hiroshima follow scenes of teachers and aid workers dealing with children of all ages, races, and colors. Shots of children with radiation poisoning show how early Craigie realized that it was not merely the bombs but the ramifications of nuclear energy programs that had to be fully investigated and controlled if there was to be a sane world and a comity of nations.

This little known film is one of Craigie's finest achievements, one in which she establishes a stimulating dialogue between images and narrators, so that her film's theme arises seamlessly out of the editing process. Hers is an idealistic view, to be sure, but one that powerfully exposes the high cost of doing nothing, of taking refuge in skepticism or cynicism, or in concentrating only on one's immediate surroundings. Through its focus on children, the film makes the world seem like a neighborhood, a community—almost a village in which the suffering of others becomes everyone's concern.

To Be A Woman

This spirit of activism also fuels the outrage expressed in *To Be a Woman*, produced by Outlook Films (William MacQuitty's company). The film opens with shots contrasting a young woman dressed in the fashion of 1950 on the way to work with a woman walking in the formal, confining dress of the late Victorian age. How do these women compare, the female narrator (Wendy Hiller) asks? How does the modern woman match up to the woman who John Stuart Mill found in a state of subjection (a subtitle reads "Women, Criminals and Lunatics May Not Vote"). "Can she develop her individual talents? Can she create the kind of society she wants?" the narrator asks during, shots of a young woman typing. "What does it mean in twentieth-century Britain to be a woman?"

During shots of women employed in various industries and businesses the narrator observes: "If anyone dares to resurrect that cliché that woman's place is in the home, let them contemplate the sight of millions of women outside of the home earning their own living." Almost a third of these women are married. Two men look askance at a woman delivery driver, prompting the female narrator to say, "Women work while men weep. Not that they've ever wept much over this [shots of a woman on her knees washing stone steps] or for that matter this [a scene of women dancing the can can]."

A male voice intrudes: "But it seems that young women with their lives before them can do what they like." Women can rise to Cabinet rank and have career and marriage at the same time, he asserts. "What more do women want?" Shots of very young, rather wistful looking girls introduce a series of statements by leaders of women's groups noting women do not have equal opportunity for training in all professions and technical specialities; they are not yet represented in large numbers in Parliament or in local government; they do not have their incomes assessed and taxed separately.

Then a cut to a woman knitting prompts the male narrator to say "Isn't she more representative of the average woman?" The knitter says she does not believe in "all this equality nonsense," and would rather stay and home and raise a family. Besides women don't like to work under women, she says. And who would employ the average woman? she asks. Her remarks are overridden by the introduction of prominent women in the arts, medicine, engineering, publishing, and trade unions, shots which in turn segue to the female narrator, who intones: "Prejudice dies hard. Sometimes it even finds quite lucid expression." Then an older man seated in a plush chair, his paunch protruding, plays "devil's advocate." It is Professor Joad, a national figure at the time who often appeared on the Brains Trust radio program with Michael Foot and other public figures. Joad argues that "on the whole" the entrance of women into the workforce has been a "mistake." The "general level of happiness," he contends, is "lower since women left their homes." Are women making great discoveries or creating great works of art or ruling countries? "Of course they're not. They are acting as drudges for the men." The female narrator counters: "But what are the facts, Professor Joad?" A shop window displays books by women, and the narrator mentions that painters like Berthe Morisot and Frances Hodgins have international reputations. A shot shows Craigie pointing at a painting in a window and arguing with her male companion. Then a shot of composer Elizabeth Lutyens follows (she composed the music for the film).

The film attacks the argument that men need higher wages than women to support their families. Shouldn't a man with a family get more than a spinster, a male voice breaks in. Well then the married man should get more than the bachelor, the female narrator responds. Less than half of the male workforce supports families. Most women are doing two jobs: taking care of home and family and teaching school or doing some other job outside the home—the scene shifts to a married man at his breakfast table while the woman is cooking and cleaning up not only for him but for an elderly gentleman, presumably her father or his. The man is getting "value and service." The wife is hardly a "dead weight."

Ian Mikardo, Michael Foot's Labour colleague in Parliament, is introduced as an industrial consultant. Mikardo explains what work costs in a factory. The way to keeps costs and prices steady is "not to pay the person doing the job but pay the job. The State looks after the extra needs which come out of the extra responsibilities of wife and children to a certain extent through family allowances, income tax rebates, and provisions for education, and the like. The same job done with the same level of skill and effort must always be paid for in the same way," he concludes.

Then the film begins its peroration, the narrator pointing out that women now staff many industries, once dominated by men. "Women are cheap labour," becomes the refrain as scenes follow of women making glass, and operating cranes, and entering new industries such as plastics and radio, where "employers hardly consider taking on men at all." The woman who sells shoes gets less than the man who sells shoes (shot of man ogling a woman clerk in a shoe store). Where there is male unemployment it has often been caused by employing women as "cheap labour. When unemployment was at its peak in Britain, the number of women employed was steadily rising." This process of undercutting male labour leads to unemployment, even when government invests in industry. "But where women are paid the rate for the job—in the BBC and in Parliament—the men are none the worse." Is a man's job safe as long as women are able to undercut the men?" The male voice intrudes again, "But all political parties agree with the principle of equal pay. But now isn't the time." The female narrator rejoins, "Now is never the time," as footage of suffragettes parading and protesting is shown. "Women were fighting for the rate for the job even before they went to prison to get the vote."

The narrator now raises her voice asking if some of the women in parliament have forgotten the "cause of women." The male interrupts "But the Chancellor of the Exchequer has told them that it will lead to inflation," to which the narrator responds: "We who represent millions of women and all political parties—civil servants, teachers, bank clerks, businesswomen and industrial workers ask: 'Would anyone of integrity mention difficulties paying him [a man with a shovel digging out a rail track] less for the job because he is a Catholic? Or him [a man stirring cement] because he is a refugee? Or him [a glassmaker] because of the color of his skin. Or him? [a man washing windows] because he has ginger hair? But we insult women in this way." The narrator points out that Britain has signed the universal declaration of human rights, which specifies equal pay for equal work. "Was this signed in good faith, or in hypocrisy?" the narrator asks. The film concludes by returning to the modern woman now leaving her employment. The narrator asks: "Isn't it time we in Britain make it a proud thing to be a woman?"

In spite of its provocative tone, Craigie's film roused little interest and was not widely reviewed. It did not have a theatrical release. She kept only one brief unidentified news item about the documentary in her papers. Later, for the television program Fifties Features, she dismissed her film as "very cheap," saying it was "not very good and I wasn't very satisfied, but I did not my best at the time." Like many of her dismissive comments about her work, this one has to be viewed with caution, since she judged herself by the highest standards, and like most artists felt disappointed when her work did not live up to her ideal conception of it. On the same program Craigie characteristically expressed pride in having employed composer Elizabeth Lutyens at the suggestion of Sir Arthur Bliss, who told her Lutyens "makes amazing sounds, you must have her." Lutyens gave her exactly the kind of "really good modern" score Craigie wanted, an intermittent, percussive aural commentary that is virtually all drumbeats, clashing cymbals, gongs, xylophone riffs, and ringing bells that reflect but also help to modulate the film's strident, impatient, imperative tone. In this film Craigie is at the end of her tether. It is a passionate, uncompromising work. It is full of good argument, but it does not have the playful, cunning tone that she so much admired in Wilde. When Michael Foot's biographer Mervyn Jones told Craigie how much he liked the film, she called it "rotten," adding I'm not proud of it." *To Be a Woman* marked, in Craigie's own mind, her final bitter effort to survive as a documentary filmmaker.

Who Are the Vandals?

Yet this is not the end of Craigie's story as a documentary filmmaker. She turned to journalism, attacking the architects who did not fulfill their promise of a "better Britain," and in articles such as "People Versus Planners," published in *The Times* (14 September 1968), she revived the spirit of '45: "If we cannot learn to challenge some of the basic assumption of city architects, if the layman is unable to intervene in the domain of the expert, the signs are that—despite all the figures of housing records—we are busy devising on a mammoth scale, a new brand of twentieth-century slum."

The radicalism of the 1960s and the election of Harold Wilson seemed to galvanize Jill and to provoke her into expressing in film and in newspaper articles her alarm that the socialist promises remained unfulfilled. She was also responding to what Terence Bendixson in *The Peterborough Effect* calls the sixties "ferment in thinking about cities. Futurism was fashionable." In 1961, Lewis Mumford had published *The City in History*, a reworking and expansion of *The Culture of the Cites*. Suddenly Craigie saw a second chance to remold the city with the same zeal that had inspired the Plymouth plan.

In 1967, she took on the Camden County Council, irritating local Labour Party leaders because of her uncompromising attack on the failures of public housing. This time it was not the war, but the planners themselves, who had destroyed the cities by putting up the monstrous tower blocks. Michael Foot remembered that Peggy Duff, a Camden councillor, attacked Craigie: "You're stopping us from building flats for people." But Craigie did not relent: In effect, the consequences of poor planning had been criminal—giving rise to the title Foot suggested for her documentary *Who Are the Vandals?* They were not the young boys marauding through the housing estates [housing projects] but the architects who had condemned whole communities to substandard housing and degrading facilities, Craigie told an interviewer:

> They think they can do it all on paper without proper consultation. They have quite a lot of mock consultation, don't they? I've been to quite a few meetings with Camden Council, where I've heard people

boo the plan, actually.... After the war architects betrayed their ethics. They had all these slogans which I fell for, because I'm a great one for falling for slogans. They used to say "A town should be for a citizen what a country estate is for a rich man: a pleasant place to walk in." Well you can's say these tower blocks [high rises] they've built with these beastly little places, all draughty, all draughty at the bottom, make pleasant places to walk in, can you?

The film, broadcast on the BBC, opens with shots of the tower blocks in the Regent's Park Estate in the north of London, with the voice over of a woman calling them "rabbit hutches." That the first voice is a woman's is important: "I saw architecture from the feminine point of view," Craigie said. "Today, I happen to think that one of the things that went most wrong with the Labour Party is its ignorance on this subject

A male voice overlaps the woman's, pointing out how the units have grown and grown, as a group of boys run wild on roofs, climbing up railings, jumping off roofs, while another male voice speaks of the damage these gangs cause, and the chaos that ensues from the unplanned consequences of building. Children parade with signs protesting the dangerous conditions in which they have no room to play and are run over by vehicles in the street.

Architect John Chisholm is shown walking into a group of women and children, introducing himself to say that he wants to talk with them about the housing scheme. He is personable, direct, and extraordinarily comfortable on camera. More than twenty years after *Out of Chaos* and *The Way We Live*, Craigie has perfected her documentary style, aided now by a handsome professional architect who has mastered the medium of television. Gone is the rigid, cadaverous look of art critic Eric Newton, the stiffness of Kenneth Clark, and the somewhat contrived scripting of the actor playing a writer returning from war who interviews the Plymouth housewives. Chisholm behaves like a man who actually practices architecture by talking to the people it is meant to house. So startled are these women to see this professional man approaching them that they ask if he is the rent collector. It is an amusing touch—indeed a wonderful demonstration of how Craigie wished to make serious points through comic encounters. Architects are so out of touch with the people that their arrival at a housing estate is a novelty. The women confirm the judgments of the voice over narrators—life in high rises is dangerous and inconvenient, with children climbing toward unsafe windows, stuck in broken elevators, and unable to play in cramped or hazardous open spaces (shots of two small boys and their mother dragging, pushing, lifting a pram up countless stairs becomes a recurrent motif in the film).

A handheld camera jerks in and out of a congestion of cars, children, bare patches of ground, and high gates as Chisholm walks to his meeting with Peggy Duff, Chairman of the planning committee in Camden Town. Chisholm is blunt. He asks her "why on earth" so many roads intersect with the playground. She explains that the recreation area was put in after the rest of the development. Chisholm is relentless, refusing to take at face value Duff's bland comment that tower blocks were simply the style that seemed appropriate after the war. He points out that there were better examples of development at the time the Tower Blocks were built. Her tone of authority is undercut by shots of boys running and jumping over balconies. A sign forbids cycling and playing games in the court-yard. In other words, there is literally no outlet for these youthful energies except the buildings themselves that the boys scale with the dexterity of jungle animals.

MP Lena Jeger interviews an articulate housewife who provides a devastating analysis of how the Regents Park estate has failed. She doubts her views would sway an architect who has his own ideas. Real change would come, she argues, only if public opinion carried more weight. The film itself, of course, is doing just that—forcing the architects to face the people. Jeger interviews another woman about the crowded conditions of a two-bedroom flat that has no room for storage and for her four children's things (the woman has been waiting for two years for a transfer to a larger flat). Chisholm then zeroes in on Brian Smith, the award winning architect for the southern part of Regent's Park. In scene after scene, Chisholm strips away Smith's defense of the Tower Blocks, exposing their bland uniformity, the lack of shopping, and the intrusion of roads into residential areas, obstructive railings, and the limited ground space. Chisholm sees sameness and standardization; Smith sees "use difference" and "visual contrast." Jeger is then heard comparing the flats in Regent's Park to the cells in a honeycomb.

As alternatives to the tower blocks, Chisholm interviews architects and shows schemes in the planning stage and also completed that provide cost efficient low-rise, high density housing schemes with a large concentrations of shopping, a landscaped public concourse, pedestrian malls, special provisions for private living spaces (including gardens and balconies). As in *The Way We Live*, Craigie's film takes the viewer step-by-step through architectural models—in this case while the architects themselves discuss the principles of planning. Architect Edward Hollamby describes his low-rise, intimate terraced housing in Lambeth that accommodates as many people as tower blocks would on the same site while suiting the scheme to existing housing (some of which is also rehabilitated). He solicits public comment—Craigie includes a scene with children questioning the architect about his provision of play area.

Craigie breaks the pattern of the film with a brief visit to William Morris's house, showing how he combined the beautiful and the practical. Hollamby says he is guided by Morris's belief in the symbiosis of the beautiful and the useful. Later in the film loving shots of the shoemaker's tools emphasize how much is lost when whole neighborhoods are demolished. Children come into a copper and brass worker's shop with metal pieces that the shop owner plates free of charge. A whole culture, in other words, is violated by the Kentish Town redevelopment scheme. "Learn to love the narrow spot that surrounds our daily life for what of beauty and sympathy there is in it," wrote William Morris, the presiding spirit of *Who Are the Vandals?*

The denouement comes in Chisholm's showdown with Kentish Town planners and councillors, chiding them for destroying the street life that supports small shopkeepers and tradesman (second hand bookshops, shoe makers, copper and brass craftsman) and evicting people from homes they cherish and only wish to improve. The argument—the back and forth between Chisholm and the three Borough representatives—carries on for a tenacious ten minutes, quite an extraordinary dialogue that few documentaries in the age of sound bites would dare to present. Chisholm does not let go, and the film ends with shot after shot of tower blocks standing in all their stark isolation while the camera rapidly tilts up and down, up and down, not only emphasizing the neck-strain of looking at these insipid cylinders but the monotony and disorientation of living in them. A plaintive, female voice sings yearningly about finding a little house of her own.

Craigie's film remains a fresh document today—a superb example of an activist film-maker constructing an argument and fomenting a sense of outrage that my documentary film students have compared to the work of their contemporary Michael Moore, another urban populist and rabble rouser. Television critic R. W. Cooper called *Who are the Vandals?* "remarkably fresh and enlightening, largely because she let people talk for themselves." (*The Times* 3 February 1967) Architects were not so happy about the film. Michael Foot remembers some threatened to sue Craigie for jeopardizing their livelihood. It disgusted her to think that architects would seek this kind of immunity, especially since, as one of them put it, they themselves are "quick to draw the gun." All the arts benefitted from criticism—as Oscar Wilde had taught her a generation ago.

Readings

Paul Rotha, *Documentary Film*

What we have come to call "documentary" did not appear as a distinctive method of filmmaking at any given moment in the cinema's history. It did not suddenly become manifest as a new conception of film in any particular production. Rather has documentary evolved over a period of time for materialist reasons; partly as the result of amateur effort, partly through serving propagandist ends, partly through aestheticism.

John Grierson, "First Principles of Documentary"

(1) We believe that the cinema's capacity for getting around, for observing and selecting from life itself, can be exploited in a new and vital art form. The studio films largely ignore this possibility of opening up the screen on the real world. They photograph acted stories against artificial backgrounds. Documentary would photograph the living scene and the living story. (2) We believe that the original (or native) actor, and the original (or native) scene are better guides to a screen interpretation of the modern world…They give it power of interpretation over more complex and astonishing happenings than the studio mind can conjure up or the studio mechanician recreate. (3) We believe that the materials and stories thus taken from the raw can be finer (more real in the philosophic sense) than the acted article.

Bill Nichols, *Introduction to Documentary*

When we believe that what we see bears witness to the way the world is, it can form the basis for our orientation to or action within the world. This is obviously true in science, where medical imaging plays a vital diagnostic role in almost all branches of medicine. Propaganda, like advertising, also relies on our belief in a bond between what we see and the way the world is, or how we might act within it. So do many documentaries when they set out to persuade us or adopt a given perspective or point of view about the world.

The underlying sense of authenticity in the film of Louis Lumière made at the end of the nineteenth century, such as *Workers Leaving the Lumière Factory, Arrival of a Train, The Waterer Watered, The Gardener,* and *Feeding the Baby,* seem but a small step away from documentary film proper. Although they are but a single shot and last but a few minutes, they seem to provide a window onto the historical world.... The departing workers in *Workers Leaving the Lumière Factory,* for example, walk out of the factory and past the camera for us to see as if we were there, watching this specific moment from the past take place all over again.

Susan Sontag, *On Photography*

In teaching us a new visual code, photographs alter and enlarge our notions of what is worth looking at and what we have a right to observe. They are a grammar and, even more importantly, an ethics of seeing. Finally, the most grandiose result of the photographic enterprise is to give us the sense that we can hold the whole world in our heads—as an anthology of images.

Erik Barnouw, *Documentary: A History of the Non-Fiction Film*

Flaherty had apparently mastered—unlike previous documentarists—the "grammar" of film as it had evolved in the fiction film. This evolution had not merely changed techniques; it had transformed the sensibilities of audiences. The ability to witness an episode from many angles and distances, seen in quick succession—a totally surrealistic privilege, unmatched in human experience—had become so much a part of the film-viewing that it was unconsciously accepted as "natural."

[*The Man With the Movie Camera*] is an essay on film truth, crammed into tantalizing ironies. But what did it finally mean for audiences? Had Vertov demonstrated the importance of the reporter or documentariest? Or had his barrage of film tricks suggested—intentionally? Unintentionally?—that no documentary could be trusted?

[The Humphrey Jennings] films are crowded with small, unspectacular moments: humorous, touching, curious. In the midst of the surrealist madness of war, they form a tapestry of men and women behaving in a human way, and somehow confirming our faith in humanity. They are carrying on. Jennings was credited with capturing the mood of the British in crisis, but he may have done more: perhaps he helped set a pattern for crisis behavior. The Jennings war films never explain, exhort, harangue. They *observe*.

Susan Sontag, "On Style"

To call Leni Riefenstahl's *The Triumph of the Will* and *The Olympiad* master-pieces is not to gloss over Nazi propaganda with aesthetic lenience. The Nazi pro-paganda is there. But something else is there, too, which we reject at our loss. Because they project the complex movements of intelligence and grace and sensu-ousness, these two films of Riefenstahl (unique among work of Nazi artists) tran-scend the categories of propaganda or even reportage. And we find ourselves—to be sure rather uncomfortably—seeing "Hitler" and not Hitler, the "1936 Olym-pics" and not the 1936 Olympics. Through Riefenstahl's genius as a filmmaker, the "content" has—let us even assume, against her intentions—come to play a purely formal role.

Susan Sontag, "Fascinating Fascism"

Fascist aesthetics include but go far beyond the rather special celebration of the primitive to be found in *The Last of the Nuba*. More generally, they flow from (and justify) a preoccupation with situations of control, submissive behavior, extravagant effort, and the endurance of pain; they endorse two seemingly oppo-site states, egomania and servitude. The relations of domination and enslavement take the form of a characteristic pageantry: the massing of groups of people; the turning of people into things; the multiplication or replication of things; and the grouping of people/things around an all-powerful, hypnotic leader-figure or force. The fascist dramaturgy centers on the orgiastic transactions between mighty forces and their puppets, uniformly garbed and shown in ever swelling numbers. Its choreography alternates between ceaseless motion and congealed, static, "virile" posing. Fascist art glorifies surrender, it exalts mindlessness, it glamorizes death.

Taylor Downing, *Olympia*

[On *Triumph of the Will*] Riefenstahl set to work with a team of 135 technicians, drivers, officials and police guards led by sixteen prominent cameramen using thirty cameras. Bridges and towers were built and tracks were laid for the cameras to move along. An enormous flagpole was equipped with an electric lift to take the cameramen to the top as the marchers fanned out below. A fire engine was requisitioned to enable a camera at the top of a 90-foot ladder to film across the rooftops. A ramp was built in the main square to allow the camera to track along with the marching troops. An airplane and airship were put at Riefenstahl's dis-posal. In a frantic whirlwind of activity Riefenstahl, then thirty-two years old, organized her teams of cameramen and sound recordists and gave them all precise instructions as to what she required.

Everything is dedicated to the worship of the leader.... The music, the rituals, the flags, the masses are all defined in terms of their relationship to the will of the Führer.... Although the stage-management of the event was itself spectacular, Riefenstahl does more than simply record the rally for posterity. She uses all her skills as a film-maker to adulate the party and worship the Führer. There is no doubt that while the film is a triumph of the cinema it is also one of the most fascistic films ever made.

[*Olympia*] Riefenstahl has always said how important it was to get the 'architecture' of the film right. Where does the film begin? Where does it end? What are its high points? What are the less dramatic events?...Most film-makers assemble a film first and then look for the rhythm and pacing to create the high and low points. Riefenstahl went the other way about it, and having given every sequence its place then worked on giving each event the pacing necessary to fit into the overall structure. She clearly saw the process of editing as being that like composing music, and wrote about cutting the film "like a symphony...according to the laws of aesthetics and rhythm."

Paul Rotha, *Documentary Film*

Triumph of the Will was unique in film history as a dramatized account of a fictional spectacle organized for propaganda...an event that for mass-parade surpassed any Hollywood super-film.

Topics for Discussion

In what sense do documentaries actually document?

How do films create their own reality?

What is the truth-value of documentaries?

Can there be such a thing as an objective documentary?

Describe the methods of an activist filmmaker.

Is there a fascist or socialist or feminist aesthetic in filmmaking?

Explore the role of montage in documentary films.

What role can rehearsal, scripting, and staging play in documentaries?

How do feature films include documentary elements?

How do documentaries include feature film elements?

Discuss Craigie's films as dialogue and Riefenstahl's as spectacle. What impact do these different approaches have on their art?

What does Riefenstahl mean by the "laws of aesthetics and rhythm"?

Discuss Jill Craigie and Michael Moore's approaches to documentary. What are pros and cons of their methods? Both produce what Paul Rotha calls "argument" films.

Five Model Film Reviews

Model 1: The "truth value" of documentaries; the role of the director; cinematic form; cinematography; the artist's body of work.

Gray's Anatomy is the third installment of actor/monologist Spalding Gray's autobiography. Of course, put that way there is the presumption that he is telling the truth about himself. And like all autobiographies, Gray's is open to question. For one thing, he is a performer, using himself as material. The material is real and yet as soon as he presents it, it becomes another story for the purposes of a film. The sly Gray, however, complicates the matter of veracity further when he remarks that the real people he becomes involved with may suspect that he is turning their stories into another quest for material. He is fictionalizing them, yet in a film, which is by definition a made-up thing, precisely calling attention to his story-making powers bolsters Gray's authenticity and that they arise out of reality, rather than being opposed to it.

Director Steven Soderbergh fruitfully extends Gray's playing with the reality/fiction nexus by beginning the film with several interviews with people who have suffered from eye problems—the malady that will be the subject of Gray's monologue. These people are not actors. The no-frills black-and-white photography emphasizes their documentary value. They tell horrendous stories without Gray's curiously suave/neurotic delivery. A woman is embarrassed to report that she mistakenly used super glue instead of eye drops, but she does not explain how such an absurd event could have occurred. Rather she relates her anxiety and the choices she faced: she could either have her eyelids surgically opened or wait several days until the glue dissolved. She elected the latter course and all was well. What is curious about her story is that it is believable precisely because it is told without any particular skill or wish to entertain. It is not a boring story because its content is arresting. How awful to be faced with such a terrifying yet also ridiculous situation. Other eye tragedies are told with even greater flatness of voice and paucity of gesture. The woodenness of these interviews is so striking that Gray's neurotic need to shape a story out of his own ailment, and the film's insistence on making a saga of his neurotic needs are brought into high and hilarious relief.

On the one hand, the interviews suggest that everyone has a story to tell. On the other hand, most stories of maladies prove to be banal—like the mechanic who matter-of-factly explains how he pulled a piece of metal out of his eye and blinded himself. His stoic and stolid narrative is in its own way stunning, the perfect foil to Gray's frenzied search for a cure to his "macular pucker," a draining away of fluid in the eye that threatens to blind him.

Gray's previous two films, *Swimming to Cambodia* and *Monster in a Box*, are brilliant monologues, but they lack his third film's cinematic form, which comments on his craziness even as he is speaking about it. Soderbergh does follow a pattern set by previous directors, though, in his use of reverse camera angles, so that Gray seems to be turning toward different members of the audience, just as one would in a conversation with more than one person. This relatively simple technique gives the film an intimate feel, as if Gray is not addressing an audience (no audience is present in the filming) but a few individuals. He could be a friend talking to other friends.

And what do friends talk about? Certainly ones that are approaching or who have surpassed fifty are concerned with their health. This is the time when various kinds of degeneration become apparent—when the fiftyish want referrals to specialists and when they seek out alternative forms of medicine when the traditional practitioners let them down. This is the period Gray calls the "Bermuda triangle" of health, a phrase his relative has coined to convey her theory that between fifty and fifty-three the individual confronts a health crisis that will determine whether or not he or she survives.

Gray's own crisis begins when he notices that his vision is blurry in one eye. He is working on a novel, and he does not want to interrupt his concentration or to contemplate the idea that there may be something really wrong with his eye. Several months later, however, the problem remains and a trip to an ophthalmologist confirms that he has a "macular pucker," a kind of bunching up of tissue where fluid has drained out of his eye. There is only a one per cent chance that the condition will correct itself—according to the officious specialist who calls Gray "Gary" and who recommends a $10,000 operation. An unnerved Gray immediately thinks of his friends who have had disastrous experiences in New York hospitals. At the very least he wants a second opinion. He consults a kinder, gentler specialist (recommended by a friend). Whereas the previous specialist said he had to "scrape" Gray's eye to correct the condition, the second one calls it "peeling," a more soothing concept to Gray. Still, Gray is hoping for some alternative to the knife. Is the operation urgent? No, the specialist replies. They can monitor the condition for a while before making the decision on an operation. And Gray is free to seek alternative solutions? He asks the specialist. Certainly, the specialist says gently, and then he can perform the operation.

Of course, both these specialists exist only in Gray's monologue—that is to say, there may have been doctors just like the ones he describes, but they have become Gray's characters performed with his trademark changes of voice and expression. Gray mocks the doctors as he mocks himself. If he is a neurotic, they seem altogether too confident about their modern specializations. Things go wrong, Gray knows, everyone knows.

This third Gray film approaches the complexity of a modern self-reflexive novel, in which the narrator interrogates his own narrative, raising questions about his grasp of reality, and of what reality means when it has to be filtered through many points of view. Only the most unimaginative minds—which include some of the documentary interviewees in the film—can treat Gray's woes as merely those of a nutty New Yorker. Not that any of these interviewees comments on Gray directly, except to say that they would not have consulted a psychic surgeon or participated in an Indian sweat lodge ceremony or gone to a nutritional ophthalmologist as Gray has done. Their reactions are hilarious because they levelly consider these alternatives and say in deadpan voices that such alternatives cures do not appeal to them.

But if the film is having fun with these rationalists who would only seek conventional treatment, it is also skewering Gray, whose shaky grasp on his identity is wonderfully revealed when two Hasidim who think he is a homeless person in need of work pick him up. They drive him to their temple in Brooklyn where he does some clean-up work, performing so well that a neighbor wants to hire him. Gray, who has never been to the Williamsburg section of Brooklyn, seems enchanted with the Hasidim and plays his role so well that he dickers with them, holding out for ten dollars instead of the eight they offer him for his work. Again, it is to be wondered if this incident occurred—or at the least if Gray is embellishing it. Further doubt is cast on the incident when he describes himself walking across the Brooklyn Bridge from Williamsburg—an impossible feat. No matter. Gray himself has already conceded that he is a storyteller. He selects/invents details that conform to the story's shape.

Quite aside from the fiction/fact tension of the film, there are Gray's musings about disease, which include the pet theories of lay men and women, the pontifications of doctors, and the spiritual and psychic healing services of alternative practitioners. Here Gray is tapping into the superstition and professionalism that pervades the culture's discussion of health. When he starts to blame himself for his illness, thinking he is being punished for an inflated ego, readers of Susan's Sontag's classic *Illness as Metaphor* will want to rise up and say a disease is a disease is a disease. It is not caused by some kind of psychic or moral sin. But that would end the film—and Gray's exploration of the sneaking feeling of the ill that they are somehow to blame for their sickness.

All this talk of disease, however, is remarkably entertaining. Gray is never less than amusing. A great talker, he can make just about anything interesting because he filters it through an exquisitely perceptive and ironic sensibility. As Henry James said, the artist must be granted his subject matter. It is how he treats it that counts, and with Gray, style is nearly all. Perfectly titled, *Gray's Anatomy* shows him to be in fine form.

Model 2: The role of photography and framing; the "look" of the image; the construction of the event; analyzing a scene; what the critics say; stylization; audience response.

Office Killer is photographer Cindy Sherman's first foray into filmmaking. Sherman is best known for her stunning series," Untitled Film Stills," which were recently exhibited at New York's Museum of Modern Art, and which attracted high praise. Sherman was deemed one of the finest artists of the past three decades. She may be the quintessential postmodernist, if what is meant by that term includes a sensibility that portrays the way contemporary identity has been largely influenced by the media, especially film and television. Indeed, Sherman's photographs treat life like a media event. She usually uses herself, posed in a scene, in a costume, in an attitude that vaguely seems to recall not a specific film but rather memories of countless films that people now imitate. Whether Sherman is some creepy clone of a movie horror victim, a gun moll, or a sex doll, it is her "acting" that is striking. Identity, in her lens, is provisional and contextual; that is, it is made up for the occasion and derives its meaning from the setting the artist chooses for herself.

Sherman's photographs are serious art, yet they are spoofs and satires. It is almost as if she is saying "how could we take the cinema so seriously when actually it is so silly, so contrived?" The photographs also suggest, however, that love of cinema is just another instance of the mimetic drive, the human impulse to create an identity out of copying and collecting images from media. Sherman's interest in freakishness and the Gothic is a latter day kind of romanticism laced with irony. Her choice of subject matter is reminiscent of that great photographer Diane Arbus, whom Susan Sontag writes about so memorably in *On Photogra-*

phy—although Arbus prefers to shoot her subject's head-on, forsaking the distorting techniques of horror films, since her subjects (dwarfs and giants, for example) simply have to present themselves in order to look freaky. Arbus seems to be employing obvious physical distortions as perhaps a metaphor for the inequalities and asymmetries of life. Sherman, on the other hand, works up her grotesqueries by means of makeup and whatever props and paraphernalia are necessary to establish a "scene." It is interesting that Sherman came to maturity as an artist at the same time as the word scenario entered into common usage via the Watergate hearings. People's stories were thought of as shooting scripts.

It is not surprising, then, that Sherman might wish to try her hand at a movie. But it is also not surprising that it has taken her a considerable time to actually produce one. There is a world of difference between films and photographs—even when the photographs are, like Sherman's, parodies of film stills. Photographs freeze a moment; they do not talk. They are enigmatic, elliptical, and fragmentary. The best photographs can repay hours of study; the multitudes of shots in a film flash by. Photographs are a static study; film is a narrative, even though it is made out of still pictures. Nevertheless, film has been such an inspiration to Sherman that she has to have wondered—as have her viewers—what she would do as a filmmaker.

Office Killer not surprisingly, has some startling visual effects. There is, for example, the scene in the photocopy room. It is late at night, and the interrupted light from the photocopy machine casts shadows. The flickering light, and the mechanical back-and-forth action of the machine, evoke a sinister, closed-in atmosphere, and a controlling environment that produces considerable tension. It seems an inhuman kind of environment in which to work, a setting in which murder is all-too-likely. It is also a place where there are no originals, where everyone is copying or following orders, desperately trying to perform on deadline and ready a magazine for press.

The film has the atmosphere of a Gothic thriller/horror film but also the mundanity the characters in Sherman's photographs are apparently escaping when they don their dramatic guises. For devotees of Sherman, there is a game to be played, identifying how close some of her movie scenes resemble her film stills. A recent article in *The New York Times* for example, juxtaposes "Untitled, No. 180), a 1987 photograph against a scene in the film when Jeanne Tripplehorn sits in shock next to two corpses. The visual echoes suggest how involved and yet how removed Sherman is from her own creations. The film scene is ghastly, but it is also laughable because it goes so over-the-top in its layering of the grotesque. There have to be two corpses, one on each side of Tripplehorn, and they have been propped up so that they seem to be watching television. This is a good joke in itself because so much ink has been wasted on deploring the zombie-like trance that television is supposed to instill in its viewers.

Actually, there are more than two corpses in the room. Dorinne (the office killer played with aplomb by Carol Kane) has begun collecting dead bodies, the result of her unfortunate, accidental killing of her boss. She has been working overtime at night, for she senses that her job is in jeopardy. She is an extremely nervous, retiring soul who is easily spooked. She has almost no friends in the office, and she is rattled because she has to learn about the new computer she has just been given. What is worse, she is trying to please a cantankerous male who ridicules her intelligence and her modest manners. Indeed, he makes her sick, and she goes to the bathroom to vomit.

On her way back to her desk, Dorinne notices that the office lights are out. She does not know that her boss has shut off the circuit breaker in order to check the connections to her malfunctioning computer. As she cautiously advances, she trips and her hands hit the circuit switch, instantly electrocuting her obnoxious boss. In shock, Dorinne tries to awaken the man. When she realizes he is dead, she takes a moment to lecture him on his bad behavior. It is a comic but enormously satisfying scene both for Dorinne and for the audience. How many times have employees wanted to have Dorinne's opportunity? The fantasy of killing off the opposition must have occurred to millions of people, even to those who do not attend horror films. It is absurd to talk to a dead person, but of course such dialogues happen all the time—and not only in the movies.

The boss's death could easily be explained, but Dorinne (so tongue-tied in the office) decides to drag the body away. She takes it home, where her invalided mother is her only company. With the boss safely dead, he becomes Dorinne's confidant. She sets him up on the sofa and flirts with him. Later she tries to straighten up and clean him with some scotch tape and Windex. Her efforts are sincere, if hilarious. Kane does not camp it up. Her Dorinne is a straightforward, dedicated worker, who proves better at her job than anyone in the company expected. Indeed, as she embarks on a crime spree, killing anyone who crosses her or who might expose her crimes, she becomes more confident and better looking, letting down her hair and using makeup. She does get carried away, though, when she does in two little girls selling girl scout cookies. (Door-to-door solicitors beware!)

Flashbacks help to explain why Dorinne is so inhibited and full of latent hostility. A good deal of it is explained when her slimy father (played expertly by Eric Bogosian) turns up in several flashbacks. He is an oily child abuser who gets his comeuppance when he tries one time too many to fondle Dorinne in the family car. The child abuse excuse should be no more than a cliché that weakens Sherman's film, but it does not because so much of the action is stylized—a comment on such explanations, not an embrace of them.

Critics have been rather hard on this film. It was held up for some time while Sherman edited and re-edited it. It has been called murky and clunky, a far cry from Sherman's sophisticated photography. Certainly the plot is unoriginal. But the performances are dead-on, with no effort to exaggerate what is by definition satirical material. A New York audience found it engrossing and entertaining—if the unusual silence and clapping afterwards count as evidence.

Office Killer is engaging because it raises questions about human identity in a sly, comic fashion. Sherman is fond of her subjects, even when she is questioning the importance we invest in them. She has real empathy for her characters, yet she retains her critical eye. Although she trades on the conventions of cinema and photographs, she also questions the suspension of disbelief we accord them. It is all rather ridiculous, her work seems to say, and yet we cannot live without these images, can we?

Model 3: Filmic structure and style; shot selection

Unzipped may be the finest film ever to reveal the gay sensibility. It is directed and designed by Douglas Keeve, a fashion photographer and Mizrahi's lover during the time of the filming. *Unzipped* is an inspired title for Douglas Reeve's documentary about Brooklyn born fashion designer Isaac Mizrahi. The film opens with Mizrahi breathlessly reading a review of one of his shows. The camera catches him the morning after in a shop where he has just purchased a paper with the fateful criticism of his work. He is devastated at the negative reaction. This is shown by the way he walks out of the shop, head bowed, and almost literally crushed as the critic's words (in a voice over of Mizrahi reading the critic's dismissal) drone on. The grainy, fuzzy black and white images emphasize the early morning hung-over world of a man of fashion with his heart on his sleeve. He is unzipped and violated by this public exposure and censure, and as the film makes abundantly clear, this is the nature of his personality. He is at one with his work, which puts him and his creations constantly on display. An extrovert, he has chosen the most extroverted of all professions, where he daily unzips and shows himself. Yet for all this constant emoting, he is never tiresomely exhibitionistic; on the contrary, his fashion-sense is courageous, moving, and always fun.

Indeed Mizrahi's response to the harsh review is to begin work on another show. The film then performs another kind of unzipping, probing the design process, observing Mizrahi test out ideas, argue with his staff, reminisce with his mother, interact with his models, and hang-out with friends like Sandra Bernhard. His enthusiasm and dedication is infectious. Even when he is hard on his staff—especially in a scene when he is informed that another designer has just publicized the idea Mizrahi has been working on—Mizrahi's own agonizing preserves our sympathy for him even as he lashes out at others.

There is plenty of anger and frustration as various items on order are late, as concepts somehow don't work out, and as the pressure mounts to produce a show that that will recapture his reputation. But Mizrahi redeems himself with a sense of humor and marvelous stories—like the one about himself at four noticing that his mother had added daisies to a plain pair of mules.

Who would have thought Isaac was watching the daisies, says Sarah Mizrahi, an obviously proud mother fascinated with her son's work.

Unzipped makes no issue of sexual preference or of the gay personality, yet Mizrahi's touching sensitivity and vulnerability, and above all his quest for style, surely make him quintessentially gay. For him, history is fashion plus sensibility; how people dress and carry themselves is not incidental or ancillary. He does not seem to be joking when he says that Mary Tyler Moore and Jackie Onassis are the most important figures of the age, the creators of the culture. This comment is then juxtaposed against a shot of the opening credits from one of Moore's television shows while Mizrahi's sings the theme song. Mizrahi's comments are funny but not frivolous; he understands how such women can move masses of people, and he is unabashed about presenting them as role models.

Part of the gay sensibility, of course, is just plain silliness. There is much ado in the film about fake fur and Mizrahi's efforts to get it to look and feel just right. A very serious fashion critic and Mizrahi confidant makes several appearances to pronounce on the fakes, paradoxically pronouncing them genuine—a wonderful epiphany of what fashion is: always a counterfeit, a Putting-on. In the fashion world people are always camping and never at home to reality.

A hilarious visit to Eartha Kitt, the sex kitten, who purrs for Mizrahi and asks him if he is going to make her gowns, rejuvenates him. Of course, he will make her gowns Mizrahi says, imitating her voice and manner just as he mimics others, just as fashion, in his hands, always mimics and thus exaggerates the world. The trip to Kitt is a defining moment in the film, for it is summative of the life in search of style. Remembering Kitt and her two poodles, Mizrahi remarks: "It's almost impossible to have style nowadays without the right dogs."

Mizrahi is so charming because he is so knowing about style without becoming cynical. Of course, fashion is manipulative and unreal. One of his favorite movies is *Call of the Wild,* in which Loretta Young, after four days of exposure to the cold, is shown in close-up with her makeup beautifully intact. "If you must freeze on the tundra, this is the way to do it," concludes Mizrahi. Of course women want to flatter themselves. "It's about women not wanting to look like cows."

Keeve brings a lover's sensibility to this film, revealing the intimate side of Mizrahi's personality (although not his love life). The film itself mimics Mizrahi's search for style by its assortment of film stocks from black-and-white to color, from16mm to 35mm, while showing clips from the designer's favorite movies. The ensemble is a kind of melding of biographical and autobiographical forms. Mizrahi is always speaking for himself, but Keeve is always the master of his medium, picking the angles and the focus (from extremely fuzzy to extremely sharp) to suit the mood of his subject and the temper of his documentary.

This is hardly just a personal film, however. There is no cloying, sentimental subtext. Mizrahi's drive is a universal artistic one; his is the energy of the creator. Even a shot of him from a home movie, in which he is like anybody's baby in a playpen, bouncing with excitement to get out, is distinctive because so much of that energy still survives in the man.

If there is a darker side to Mizrahi, if he throws prolonged tantrums or abuses people, that has been edited out of the film, or perhaps was never shown to the camera. There is one moment when Mizrahi is planning to use a transparent scrim for his show, so that the audience will be invited to get a glimpse of his models preparing for their performances. An aghast staff member cautions him that the models may not agree to this kind of exposure. Tough, is Mizrahi's reply—so caught up is he in the concept. In fact, we then seem him tentatively proposing the idea to several models, meekly accepting their rebuffs or querulous responses. He knows he's asking a lot of them. Keeve builds suspense around this element. Will the show have a scrim?

How will it be possible for some models to agree to this exposure and others not?

But the battle over the scrim is not merely a clever plotting device; it is at the heart of Mizrahi's fashion sense. He knows that people want a good show. They want to watch the models parade down the runway, lights flashing, music pounding. When *Unzipped* culminates in just such a scene, the documentary has given way completely to Mizrahi's world, the world of Hollywood films and glamorous women, flawless makeup and perfect bodies moving against and with fabric—indeed an entirely fabricated world. It is a stunning moment—watching not only the models but also the stars watching the models. Roseanne is there; so is

Sandra Bernhard, Richard Gere (then married to Cindy Crawford, one of Mizrahi's models). Stars are watching stars and they glitter among each other. What makes this scene work is the scrim, the sense of backstage life. The audience can almost peer through the gauzy fabric that separates the stage and runway from them. They are the privileged voyeurs of the fashion-process. They are getting a purchase not merely on a season's fashions but on the creative moment itself, unzipped, so to speak.

This final scene, in other words, is really a recapitulation of the whole film. There it is: the show itself and the making of a show, the shooting of the film and the film itself. The filmmaker's and his subject's sensibilities fuse in a work of art, a work of love.

There does not seem to be a superfluous shot in this 76minute movie. It is difficult to imagine it being a second longer or shorter. When Mizrahi reads the rave review the next day, bringing the film full circle, it not only completes the documentary; it describes the fashion cycle, from show to show, from one creative moment to the next. The next one may be a triumph, or it may be a disaster. Either way Mizrahi will be unzipped, having only something like that scrim, the most fragile of shields, to protect him even as it reveals his personality and his art.

Model 4: Historical context; comparative analysis; fiction and nonfiction films.

The Long Way Home won an Academy Award for the best documentary in 1997. Sponsored by the Simon Wiesenthal Center, the film begins with extraordinary documentary footage of the Nazi concentration camps, but then it segues into a lesser known story about the fate of camp survivors and the drive to establish the state of Israel.

To assess *The Long Way Home's* unique power, it is useful to describe other cinematic treatments of the Holocaust and its aftermath. One of the earliest and best films is French director Alan Resnais's *Night and Fog.* (1956). He interspersed scenes (shot in color) of the camps in the 1950s with black-and-white photographs and newsreel footage taken soon after the inmates were liberated from their horror. Resnais's cinematographer probed camp sites relentlessly in tracking shots that seemed to evoke the postwar effort to comprehend the monstrosity of the recent past. Even ten years after World War II, the full dimensions of the Holocaust were not well known and certainly not confronted in Europe or in America—in spite of the appearance of eyewitness accounts such as Primo Levi's *Survival in Auschwitz* (1959), Elie Wiesel's *Night* (1960), and Victor Frankl's *Man's Search For Meaning* (1962). In *Exodusv* (1960), starring Paul Newman and Eva Marie Saint, director Otto Preminger was one of the few Hollywood filmmakers who attempted to dramatize the aftermath of the Holocaust and the founding of the state of Israel. This stirring film concentrates on the heroism of Zionists, who triumph over a seemingly overwhelming number of Arabs. More typical of Hollywood film was *The Diary of Anne Frank* (1959), based on the Broadway play that emphasized the fate of Anne and her family in universal terms, downplaying their Jewish identities.

Most films, in Europe and in America, did not address the historical context in which the Holocaust was created. Exceptions were the French director, Marcel Ophuls, whose documentary, *The Sorrow and the Pity* (1971) presented a searing look at French society and those who collaborated with the Nazis in making the world of the camps possible. Similarly, French director Claude Lanzmann employed his documentary *Shoah* (1985) to probe the complicity of the Poles and others in setting up the camps and in creating an atmosphere in which millions of lives perished.

Two other American films should be mentioned, though, in creating a context for an appraisal of *The Long Way Home*. The television miniseries *Holocaust*(1978) tried to make the horrors of the Holocaust comprehensible in terms of individuals and families, just as and *Roots* attempted to make the Middle Passage and slavery an intimate, accessible experience. Neither of these films could escape the sentimentality and simplistic plot structures of the commercial television medium. Similarly, director Steven Spielberg's epic film, *Schindler's List*, while evoking a good deal of the trauma and human waste of the Holocaust, could not avoid reducing this historical tragedy into the factitious formulas of Hollywood product.

The Long Way Home seems conscious of the strengths and weaknesses of previous efforts to picture the Holocaust and its consequences. Writer and director Mark Jonathan Harris selects for the beginning of his film documentary footage that goes beyond the usual depiction of the concentration camp *victims—their* emaciated bodies, corpses piled in shallow trenches, and cadaverous figures clinging to wire fences. Such shots are in his film, but so are scenes of camp inmates fighting over food that their rescuers are trying to distribute. American soldiers stare at the inmates in incomprehension, sometimes with sympathetic looks, sometimes with barely concealed disgust.

The Long Way Home makes clear that many Americans did not understand what they were seeing. General George Paton thought of the inmates as animals and did nothing to conceal his anti-Semitism. When General Eisenhower visited the liberated camps under Paton's command, he was so outraged at the poor treatment of the survivors that he had Paton removed from his post.

In its first thirty minutes, the film employs professional actors to read from the diaries and letters of concentration camp survivors. Neither the actors nor the actual survivors appear on camera. Instead, as in the Resnais film, the camera roams ceaselessly over concentration camp sites as if trying to match the survivors' words to the hellish places that confined them. By withholding shots of present-day survivors and of the camps as they appear today even as voices of the survivors play over the documentary footage, a tremendous sense of yearning is created, a desire to somehow make contact with the reality that the words and the documentary footage represent. The film makes its audience into searchers of its scenes, so that when the director finally does begin to intercut the documentary footage with scenes of present-day survivors, there is an enormous relief—as if all the previous viewing of the remnants of the past has earned viewers the right to see the survivors.

Harris's accomplishment is extraordinary, because he has found a means to honor the past and the sense that it cannot be recaptured while at the same time creating an obsessive need to find out what happened, to see the people who carried on from that seemingly hopeless point, when what they had gone through was understood by almost no one, and when the energy (physical and moral) to retell the story hardly existed.

Out of this despair that the world would never understand, the camp survivors and other Zionists persisted in their drive to create the state of Israel. If Paton was an egregious example of the prejudice and ignorance that the survivors faced, there were nevertheless plenty of others in power who wanted no part in creating a homeland for the Jews. Jews will never be safe, Zionists argued, until they had their own ancestral land.

Much of the remaining part of *The Long Way Home* is about the story of a people re-creating themselves, and it has as much right to tell that story as present-day Palestinians would have a right to make a documentary about their camps and displacements. And the fact is that the plight of the Jews, what they continued to suffer in the camps after World War II, would have been ignored if not for Zionist agitation. Gifted with great political leaders such as David Ben Gurion and Abba Eban (interviewed in the film), the Zionists were able to enlist the United States and, most surprisingly, the Soviet Union as the crucial deciding votes in the United Nations that led to the creation of the state of Israel 1948.

In some ways, the greatest hero in the film is President Harry Truman. One of his closest advisors, Clark Clifford, is filmed explaining Truman's single-minded support for the idea of Israel. Clearly a dying man, Clifford speaks in a barely audible but firm whisper, recalling Truman's enormous courage and decisiveness.

His major advisors, except for Clifford, argued against recognizing Israel. George Marshall, then in Truman's cabinet and the architect of the famous Marshall Plan that did so much to rebuild Western Europe, told his President point-blank that if he did not change his position on Israel, Marshall would not be able to vote for him in the next election. But Truman did not waver.

Of course Truman was lobbied by Zionist leaders (a part of the story the film does not tell). Yet many American Jews also opposed the creation of the state of Israel, some believing that assimilation was inevitable, while certain Orthodox Jews believed Israel would come into existence only upon the arrival of the Messiah. What is more, Truman was hardly responding to a groundswell of support for the idea of Israel. Ernest Bevin, who was restricting Jewish immigration to Palestine and turning away Jews who showed up in boats in their promised land, pointed out that America had its own restrictive policies on immigration.

The Long Way Home takes an unabashedly pro-Zionist point of view. It spends virtually no time considering the plight of the Arabs (not yet called Palestinians) who occupied land that Zionists wanted for their state. At the same time, it does not blink at the fact that Zionists used terror to create the state of Israel, eventually forcing the British out of Palestine.

But the film does not discount how dispirited many of the Jewish concentration camp survivors were. Some died shortly after liberation, literally eating themselves to death after years of starvation. Others could not bring themselves to share the horror of their experience with their families—if they had any families left. Yet many of those who felt their lives were broken beyond repair continued to have children in the abysmal conditions of refugee camps. Ruth Gruber, an American newspaper correspondent, realized that though "their world was gone, "they had to continue for their children." The film's narrator, the distinguished actor Morgan Freeman, speaking for these survivors, concludes: "The world lost, and yet we won. We are going on."

Model 5: Documentary as Biography; fiction and nonfiction film

Anne Frank Remembered is a moving documentary of the life and death of an adolescent Jewish girl and budding writer. Few people who know anything about the Holocaust have not heard about her story or read her diary. In addition to a stage play and movie based on her diary, there have been countless discussions of her writing. She has been a symbol of history for more than two generations. It might seem that there is little more to be said, and that another movie is not needed to honor her legacy and probe her fate.

But the poignancy of Anne Frank's own words, and the fact that her whole diary has only just been published, ensure that she will remain a fascinating and haunting figure. In a sense, she has been rediscovered, with the previously censored portions of her diary revealing her growing awareness of her sexuality and her fierce individuality. She seems a less sheltered and innocent figure, and a more complex human being.

Some years ago Philip Roth published a novel, *The Ghost Writer*, imagining what Anne Frank's life would have been like had she survived the concentration camps. She is a compelling subject for writers because she wanted to be a writer and saw her diary as a literary contribution to an understanding of her time. She has become, in other words, not only a Holocaust figure, emblematic of the Jews who perished, but also a type of the struggling, articulate soul, of the individual who craves recognition and even fame. Anne Frank was unique because she wanted much more than her family's or her friends' or her community's acknowledgement. In the uncompromising way of youth she wanted the world to pay attention. Part of the grief she evokes is for the annihilated artist.

Anne Frank Remembered tells her story through the words and visual expressions of those who knew her and through her family photographs. What emerges is a much less sentimental story than the filmed and stage versions of her life. Anne was the spoiled daughter, doted on by her father and ineffectually disciplined by her mother. Anne could be a showoff and a know-it-all. As one of her friends' mothers said, God knew everything, but Anne knew it better. Anne seemed born with the writer's cruel streak, a self-absorbed and self-regarding sensibility that led her to treat others contemptuously—especially if they seemed lacking in imagination.

Anne was also ebullient and great fun to be with. The witnesses to her life, especially men, were charmed by her insouciance. She was a precocious adolescent full of wonder about her developing body—and a little frustrated that she had no one who could really talk to her about it. She found her comfortable, middle class home rather stuffy, and no one—not even her adoring father—ever knew just how much of her life was a kind of secret that needed the vessel of writing for its expression.

Had it not been for the Holocaust, Anne's story would not have been remarkable: a rebellious teenager, intolerant of the adult world, yearning to be a writer. But her quest to be free fused with world historical events that at first overwhelmed her family but which ultimately became the story of her tragedy and her triumph. As a writer she was handed material by fate, and she did not for a moment hesitate to capitalize on her terrible yet magnificent opportunity.

The Franks were a Jewish family—not particularly religious—that had moved from Germany to Holland when the Nazis seized control in 1933. Otto Frank had served in the German army in World War I, and it pained him to leave a country he had loyally served and loved. Because Holland had escaped the ravages of World War I, Frank was certain he had brought his family to a secure refuge. Only at the last minute, realizing the Nazis would invade all of the Low Countries, did he manage to sequester his family on the upper floors of a building where they were supposed to wait out the war until the Allies liberated them.

At first Anne responded exuberantly to her incarceration. She was intensely lonely, but her diary (a birthday gift) provided an outlet. Indeed, she realized she could speak to the diary as her friend in a way that she could never actually confide in a real-life girlfriend. In other words, Anne Frank discovered her literary vocation, inventing a friend and even answering that invented friend's letters. The diary became Anne's epistolary novel and the vehicle for her faith in the future—that somehow her words would make it out of her attic and into the world. Indeed, she became the very legend of the writer creating a life's work in a garret.

Cooped up and having to share her bedroom with an older man, a dentist whom Otto Frank's friends had asked Otto to hide, Anne lashed out. She found the dentist a dolt, her mother devoid of imaginative sensitivity, and even the adolescent boy to whom she at first confided in almost like a lover to be a dullard. The temperamental Anne vented her feelings in her diary, gradually seeing it, however, not merely as an exercise of her ego but as a work of literature that she began to rewrite as if for publication.

In *Anne Frank Remembered*, the story of Anne's growing self-consciousness and sense of isolation is corroborated by her girlfriends and the family's supporters both before and during the war. Both the authenticity of the diary and the validity of many of Anne's judgments are secured in this testimony. At the same time, the profundity of Anne's character eluded them, for it was only fully expressed in the diary. Otto Frank would say many years later that he thought he had known his daughter quite well but that the diary revealed a person he had not really known at all. The poignancy of his statement makes Anne an even greater symbol of the mystery of individuality and of how precious and unique one life can be.

Although *Anne Frank Remembered* does full justice to the period of the Frank family's confinement in the attic, it deviates from the stage and film versions of her life by spending nearly as much time on what happened to Anne and her family after they were betrayed to the Nazis. Interviews with camp survivors who befriended Otto Frank and his daughters (Anne's older sister Margo receives the least attention of all family members) make it possible to piece together those harrowing last days. Indeed, interview after interview recreates the feeling of a tragic story slowly revealing itself.

Ripped from their hiding place, packed into cattle cars, and dumped into the concentration camp, the Franks solidified. Several witnesses report that the tensions between Anne and her mother dissolved. There were as one in their suffering. Otto Frank remained in the camp what he had been all his life: a stalwart patriarch devising ways of surviving and triumphing over vicissitude. He counseled one camp inmate, Sal de Liema, to avoid a group of men obsessing about food. In their weakened condition these starving men would surely succumb if they remain fixated on their hunger. Instead, Otto advised his friend to think about music and the great composers, or about the museums he had visited or anything that would take his mind off the camp and his present condition. In a revealing moment, Otto asked de Liema to call him Papa Frank. De Liema replied that he had a father whom he knew to be safely hidden from the Nazis. De Liema supposed that Otto was trying to bolster him. But Otto replied that it was for his own benefit that he asked Sal to call him papa. Otto Frank's identity was as a father, and he could not live without it. To the end of Otto's life, Sal continued to address him as Papa Frank.

Anne's story in the camps is unbearable, but the camp survivors tell it simply and with great dignity. One of her friends, Hanneli Goslar, discovered that Anne was living on the other side of a barbed wire fence at Bergen-Belsen, and the two friends shouted to each other at night. Anne told Hanneli that Margo was dying. Anne's mother had already died of starvation and exhaustion, and Anne was ill—first with scabies and then most likely with typhoid. Because of illness she had missed a transport that would have taken her to a labor camp, where she probably would have survived the war. She died only a month before Bergen-Belsen was liberated.

After the war Otto Frank searched for his daughters for seven years before finally learning of their horrible fate. It was only then that his great friend, Miep Gies, who had worked for Otto and visited the family every day in their hiding place (a great act of heroism, but only one of several this courageous woman performed), told him of Anne's diary. It had been dumped out of Otto's briefcase by a Nazi officer who found the briefcase of more value than the diary, and Miep had recovered the diary the next day from the apartment's floor. Miep did not tell Otto of the diary's survival until Otto was certain of Anne's death. Why? She does not explain. But she does say that she did not read the diary—apparently safeguarding Anne's privacy as she had tried to protect her life. This is a great story of human integrity and the power of the word.

Classic Documentaries on VHS and DVD

Anne Frank Remembered

The Atomic Cafe

Bowling for Columbine

Brother's Keeper

Capturing the Friedmans

The Celluloid Closet

The Civil War (Ken Burns)

Crumb

The Day After Trinity

The Endless Summer

Farenheit 9/11

The Fog of War

42 Up

Frank Lloyd Wright (Ken Burns)

Gray's Anatomy

Hearts and Minds

Listen to Britain and other Films by Humphrey Jennings

The Long Way Home

Louisiana Story

The Lumière Brothers' First Films

Man of Aran

Man with the Movie Camera

Nanook of the North

Night and Fog

The Olympiad

Pumping Iron

Roger & Me

The Rolling Stones: Gimme Shelter

Rosie the Riveter

Sherman's March

Shoah

Swimming to Cambodia

The Times of Harvey Milk

Triumph of the Will

Unzipped

The War Room

When We Were Kings

Why We Fight

Index

0-595-33925-5

Printed in the United States
46065LVS00003B/141

9 780595 339259